The Equal Rights Amendment: The Politics and Process of Ratification of the 27th Amendment to the U.S. Constitution

Now the time is ripe for the women to step in and take hold of conditions. . . In these times of unrest we need women of the type of Harriet Tubman and Sojourner Truth. Women of mental ripeness, courage and clearness of purpose and a burning spirit to dare and to do. . . We need women who will not sell their rights for a mess of pottage. We need women who will not follow blindly a party because of its name, women who will break away from any party that does not stand for absolute equality of opportunity for each and every human being. . . Oh! where are you women of courage? Step out into the battle. Those of you who want the best things in life for all human-kind—you who yearn for that social justice without which the advent of the brotherhood of man is a myth—step out!. . .

> Mrs. Robert M. Patterson, ''The
> Negro Woman in Politics,'' in
> *Women's Voice*, 3 (September 1922),
> reprinted in *Black Women in White
> America: A Documentary History*,
> ed. Gerda Lerner (New York: Vintage
> Books, 1973), pp. 341–42.

The Equal Rights Amendment: The Politics and Process of Ratification of the 27th Amendment to the U.S. Constitution

Sarah Slavin, Symposium Editor

Women & Politics
Volume 2, Numbers 1/2

The Haworth Press
New York

Women & Politics, Volume 2, Numbers 1/2, Spring/Summer 1982.

Women & Politics is published quarterly in Spring, Summer, Fall and Winter. Articles in this journal are selectively indexed or abstracted in *International Political Science Abstracts* and the *Pais Bulletin*.

BUSINESS OFFICE. All subscription and advertising inquiries should be directed to The Haworth Press, 28 East 22 Street, New York, NY 10010. Telephone (212)228-2800.

SUBSCRIPTIONS are on a calendar year, per volume basis only. Payment must be made in U.S. or Canadian funds only. $28.00 individuals, $48.00 institutions, and $65.00 libraries. Postage and handling: U.S. orders, add $1.75; Canadian orders, add $6.00 U.S. currency or $6.50 Canadian currency. Foreign orders: individuals, add $20.00; institutions, add $30.00, libraries, add $40.00 (includes postage and handling).

CHANGE OF ADDRESS. Please notify the Subscription Department, The Haworth Press, 75 Griswold Street, Binghamton, NY 13904 of address changes. Please allow six weeks for processing: include old and new addresses, including both zip codes.

ISSN: 0195-7732.

Second-class postage paid at New York, NY and at additional mailing offices.

POSTMASTER: Send changes of address to The Haworth Press, 28 East 22 Street, New York, NY 10010.

The Haworth Press, Inc., 10 Alice Street, Binghamton, NY 13904-1580

Library of Congress Cataloging in Publication Data

Main entry under title:

The Equal Rights Amendment.

    (Women & politics ; v. 2, no. 1/2)
    Includes bibliographies.
    1. Sex discrimination against women–Law and legislation–United States.
2. Women–Legal status, laws, etc.--United States. 3. United States--Constitutional law--Amendments--Ratification. I. Slavin, Sarah. II. Series.
HQ1236.W63 vol. 2, no. 1/2 [KF4758]   82-9340
ISBN 0-917724-86-0   320'.088'042s   [342.73'0878]
              320'.088'042s   [347.302878]

Women & Politics

The Equal Rights Amendment: The Politics and Process of Ratification of the 27th Amendment to the U.S. Constitution

Volume 2
Numbers 1/2

Contents

MANUSCRIPTS should be submitted in triplicate with a 100 word abstract to the Editor, *Women & Politics*, Sarah Slavin, Economics and Political Science Department, State University College at Buffalo, 1300 Elmwood Avenue, Buffalo, NY 14222. Information regarding manuscript submission and a brochure, ''Information for Authors,'' are available upon request from the Editor. *Books for review purposes* should be submitted to the Book Review Editor, Sharon L. Wolchik, Institute for Sino-Soviet Studies, Department of Political Science, The George Washington University, Washington, DC 20052.

When this double-issue was in preparation, the move to ratify the equal rights amendment had begun to look less than promising and the move not to ratify, more than promising. Each movement presents us with living examples of women in politics, with assertions by women on behalf of their beliefs--ideologically and, I believe, in self as well. Suffice to say, the political beliefs at issue are examples of women's diversity. The struggle for the ERA, at the time of this writing (June 11, 1982), appears to be lost and the struggle against it, to be won. As a ratification supporter, I am of course dissatisfied with the immediate outcome of this struggle. I agree with Ellie Smeal, President of National Organization for Women, that there will always be a need for equal rights for women, and for other oppressed groups in our society. I agree with my mother, Ruth Martin Slavin, that we will begin to achieve equal rights. Nonetheless, as managing editor of *Women & Politics*, my intention is to be even-handed in the publication of materials about women and politics. While the introduction to this particular issue is written by Susan S. Shear, Missouri state representative and ERA supporter, the introduction is one among many that could have been written. We have scheduled for future publication an issue focusing largely on right-wing women. I am seeking a right-wing woman to introduce that issue. My hope is that our various advocacies will not overcome the need we share to find connections between women and to understand the diversity among women that contributes to our differences. We have scheduled for future publication an issue focusing on this need: it will be a very diverse issue and, on its face, conflictual. In that issue, as in this one, we need to "read between the lines." I think the same may be said for all issues of *Women & Politics*. --Sarah Slavin, Editor

INTRODUCTION

It was over 50 years ago that the equal rights amendment was first introduced in Congress. The amendment was finally passed by an overwhelming majority in March of 1972 and sent to the states for ratification. Almost immediately, 22 states ratified it. Now, more than eight years later, we are still three states short of ratification, stymied by a few legislators who are unwilling to grant everyone a constitutional guarantee of equality under the law. How have we reached this impasse? Why was it necessary for Congress to vote an extension of time for ratification until June 30, 1982?

We need, I submit, a constitutional guarantee of equal rights under the law. It was not until November, 1971, that the Supreme Court decided for the first time that sex discrimination violated the equal protection clause of the U.S. Constitution (*Reed v. Reed*). However, the opinion indicated that the only justification needed to discriminate by sex was a "rational basis." If a respectable body, knowledgeable in a particular area, chooses to discriminate, it is still all right to do so. The Court has continued to rule on sex discrimination cases but has been reluctant to rule that classifications based on sex are "inherently suspect—subject to the strictest judicial scrutiny" as it has ruled on classifications based on race.

Numerous barriers to justice for women remain in federal and state laws as well as administrative practices. For instance, just recently in Missouri a state employees' retirement plan required equal contributions by both men and women, but the women received almost $100 per month less than the men in pensions. This disparity has been challenged before the Human Rights Commission by 16 of the 19 women members of the Missouri legislature. If we had the equal rights amendment such practices would be outlawed.

It has been estimated there are approximately 800 federal laws that discriminate. For example, sex discrimination is written into the federal inheritance laws. A wife's labor in her own home, on the family farm or within the family business counts for nothing unless she has also made a monetary contribution. To give some examples of state laws that discriminate—in Arkansas and Louisiana homemakers are denied equal property rights with

1

their husbands. In South Dakota and Georgia a husband can disinherit his wife. In New York a wife can be sued for desertion if she refuses to follow her husband when he moves and also if he refuses to follow her when she moves.

· Further, even if these laws were repealed, we are still at the mercy of changing legislatures. The laws could be reinstated—and have been in the past. That is why, in my estimation, a constitutional guarantee is needed.

As everyone knows, ERA opponents have been extremely vocal. They have convinced four state legislatures to rescind their ratification of ERA and are constantly working for rescission in other states that have ratified. They now have a new tactic—declaring a state's ratification "null and void" since March 23, 1979, the original deadline for ratification. In the last round of legislative sessions alone, proponents managed to defeat eight rescission attempts and seven null-and-void bills.

The opponents center their opposition on the claim that ERA will lead to a breakdown of the family, the assumption being that denying women equal legal rights somehow leads to more stability in families. As a matter of fact, even without ERA, divorce is on the increase. Conditions in a rapidly changing society might account for this, but just maybe the passage of the equal rights amendment with its guarantee of legal equality might be a way to combat this downward trend and strengthen the family. It is surely worth trying.

There are, in my opinion, three kinds of women who oppose the amendment, First, the Queen Bee, who believes she has made it to the top the hard way and that all other women should do the same. She has a vague notion that the ERA might mean competition, and her insecurity in a so-called man's world makes her an opponent of the amendment. Then there is the ravishing beauty who has gotten everything she wants and does not want to "rock the boat." She likes the situation the way it is and doesn't want to take the chance of any government action that might change the status quo. And there is the homemaker whose status would be enhanced with the passage of the amendment but who has been frightened to death by anti-ERA hysterics.

The opposition defends discriminatory laws if they ostensibly benefit women. They want to retain laws that proscribe a husband's obligation to support his wife. They do not believe a wife should be liable for support if her husband is physically or otherwise unable to take on this responsibility.

The ERA would require that both sexes have the right and the responsibility to defend our country. The opponents rejoice that the Supreme Court has refused to make sex, like race and religion, a suspect classification under the fourteenth amendment, because otherwise women would no longer be the beneficiaries of laws that prevented them from being drafted and sent to combat and possibly captured as prisoners of war. There is an implication here that this is all right for our sons—but not our daughters. Former President Carter has said that as Commander-in-Chief of our armed forces, he has seen, firsthand, the tremendous benefit derived in all of the military forces from the service of women.

Is the pen mightier than the sword? The media have given credence to the fringe elements of both sides of the issue and have capitalized on the emotionalism of it rather than on rational reasoning. The media also often promote sex stereotypes and tell girls and boys that their lives must be based on sexuality. Sex is used to sell everything from soap to automobiles. And few complain that we deny constitutional rights to more than one-half of the population because of sex.

The bottom line is green—money! Have we really learned to play "hard ball?" A case in point is what happened in 1979 in Illinois, when charges of bribery were leveled against ERA proponents—that they were attempting to buy votes for ERA in the state legislature. A great hue and cry was raised but there was no attempt to level similar charges against the anti-ERA people, even though it is common knowledge that they have made vast campaign contributions to opponents of ERA for years.

Our last best hope lay in the 1980 elections, which were over and done before this issue of *Women & Politics* was published. Will the proponents now be able to effect enough changes to get the few additional votes necessary for ratification? What will happen if the amendment doesn't pass? Will it go away? I believe the answer is a resounding no! Sooner or later the lawmakers in this country will realize that the citizens want equal rights guaranteed in the Constitution along with freedom of speech, freedom of the press and freedom of religion, and that we will not settle for anything less.

I am a new grandmother, and I want my granddaughter to grow up in a world where the legal rights and responsibilities of all persons are shared equally and recognized as the law of the land.

The Honorable Susan S. Shear,
Member of the Missouri State
House of Representatives

SYSTEMIC FACTORS UNDERLYING LEGISLATIVE RESPONSES TO WOMAN SUFFRAGE AND THE EQUAL RIGHTS AMENDMENT

Janet K. Boles

ABSTRACT. This article uses a variety of quantitative data in the comparative analysis of state legislative responses to woman suffrage and the equal rights amendment. Despite the fifty years separating their adoptions, the correlates of passage for each measure were quite similar. A model of policy innovation on women's equity issues was then tested by using legislative actions on the ERA alone. Findings indicate that decisions on the ERA in the states are related to: political culture, the state's history of policy making on similar issues, and contemporary political and socioeconomic environments. Finally, a comparison of the political and intellectual antecedents of the two amendments suggests reasons for differences in the speed of their adoption in the states.

The American political system has long tolerated a major societal paradox: widespread belief in the principle of equity alongside vast status differences among the population. This gap between ideology and outcomes, however, has increasingly become the source of heavy demands for equity policies and practices. These demands have extended far beyond the economic realm to include matters of racial, ethnic, and sexual equity. There is awareness that the prejudice of individuals cannot fully explain the status of racial and ethnic minorities and women. Instead, it is believed that the legal codes, informal rules, and roles of society (i.e., institutionalized racism/sexism) maintain patterns of discrimination directed against these groups.

During this century, the federal government and the states have adopted or considered a number of policies, including two amendments to the U.S. Constitution, directed toward achieving equity between the sexes. This article uses a variety of quantitative data in the comparative analysis of state

Janet K. Boles is an Assistant Professor, Department of Political Science, Marquette University, Milwaukee, WI 53233. This is a revised version of a paper presented at the annual meeting of the Western Political Science Association, San Francisco, 1980.

5

legislative responses to these two constitutional amendments: woman suffrage and the equal rights amendment.

It is a common practice of the media to treat women-related issues as though they form a monolithic group of policies. Further, social scientists have criticized the use of a simple, additive index based on several such policies.[1] Such a measure assumes an interrelatedness which is not empirically demonstrated.[2] Therefore, I would emphasize that the treatment of these two women-related issues within a common analytical framework does not challenge findings regarding the multidimensionality of public and legislative responses to women's public policy issues.[3] Previous research has established that the determinants of policy outputs vary within an area just as they vary between policy areas.[4] Many public policies are also internally multidimensional. A single policy may fall within different categories at different points in the policy process; and different legislators may perceive the same issue differently at a single point. Even so, shared patterns of policy making in the states do exist.[5] I expected to find such a pattern for the two issues studied here.

Decision Making on Woman Suffrage and the ERA

The rationale for a comparative analysis of woman suffrage and the ERA is based on several striking parallels between the two policies. Neither, at the time of Congressional passage, could be termed new policies; both required a germination period of approximately fifty years.[6] Both grew out of a broader social movement for women's rights which came to focus on their passage. As reflected in the public and legislative controversies surrounding both, each amendment has economic, moral and civil rights dimensions. Given a strict reading of Congressional intent, however, both would appear to be civil rights issues which deal with role equity. The nineteenth amendment provided women a basis for virtual political representation and influence commensurate with men; the ERA will provide women with a similar basis for equal treatment before the law. Finally, there is a strong positive relationship between ratification of the ERA and of suffrage (Phi = .49), based on the rejection of both amendments in eight states of the Deep South.

The initial purpose here was simply to discover similarities, if any, between the socioeconomic and political correlates of legislative responses to the two amendments. Given this focus on common patterns of decision making, questions of causality or of the primacy of any particular type of factor in the two decisions are not pertinent. Although exploratory in nature, this approach offers a necessary, manageable, albeit limited step toward understanding responses to women-related policies in the American states.

I treated the direction of legislative responses to the two amendments as a dichotomous dependent variable: passage or rejection. I also used a more precise indicator of legislative support to distinguish those states which overwhelmingly favored the amendments from those which offered major opposition. This measure of legislative consensus was the percentage of the legislature present and voting for the amendment.[7]

Three types of independent variables appear in the analysis: socioeconomic, political and status of women. In general, I expected that the passage of these two amendments would be jointly related to a variety of socioeconomic and political characteristics of the states. To maximize the validity of the relationships found between these dependent and independent variables, all measures are from a common time period close to the policy decision itself.[8] The appendix provides a complete list of variables with sources.

The socioeconomic environment, even when narrowly defined as in the present study, is an important determinant of public policy because it is a major source of constraints on the choices available to decision makers. Socioeconomic variables indicating the relative urbanism of the population were: total population, population density and percent urban residence. In addition, I used three measures of the socioeconomic status of the states' population: per capita personal income, education and industrial employment.

I expected that those variables which reflect a large, complex, affluent and well-educated urban society would be strongly related to passage of the amendments. That is, I hypothesized a positive relationship between all six independent variables and the dependent variables. This would merely support previous findings that these characteristics are associated with higher levels of services and the ability to adopt new programs somewhat more rapidly.[9] A linkage also exists between a well-educated and urban population and tolerance and liberal social welfare policies, both of which lead to a prediction of more equal legal treatment of women and men. Further, complex industrial society tends to weaken traditional sex roles and is also associated with the passage of civil rights legislation,[10] two factors again which should facilitate equity between the sexes.

Social scientists traditionally view political variables as mediating factors which translate public demands for policies as accurately as possible. Indicators of mass political behavior used here were: voting participation, party competition, party control of the legislature and Democratic vote.

Because both major political parties had formally endorsed the amendments at the time passage was attempted, I expected that legislative party would have no relationship to passage within a state. There is some evidence, however, that parties engaged in closely contested elections are more eager to enact new and progressive programs in order to compete for all groups' approval.[11] Therefore I expected the level of inter-party competition to be positively related to passage. Since there are a larger number of one-party Democratic states than there are states with Republican hegemony, I predicted an inverse relationship between passage and percent Democratic vote. Finally, I hypothesized a positive relationship between voting participation and passage, based on the assumption that a participatory political system is one in which members of lower-status groups (including women) that normally are less likely to vote are able to effectively press demands for equity policies.

Because both amendments encountered their strongest opposition in the South,[12] I included a dummy variable for Southern regionalism which I expected to be inversely related to passage. Given the persistence of regional patterns of policy innovation,[13] I also used Southern regionalism as a control variable.

Since the purpose of both amendments was to improve the political or legal status of women, I was also interested in the relationships between certain indicators of the social status of women and legislative responses to the two amendments. Variables here included: marital status, sex ratio, fertility rate, education and labor force participation among white married women.[14]

The opponents of both amendments frequently presented themselves as guardians of the traditional role of women as full-time wives and mothers. The extension of equal legal rights and the vote to women, they argued, would bring the downfall of home, church and the state. These anti-feminist arguments logically would be less effective in states where an above-average percentage of women had broken with this traditional role. Therefore, I expected those characteristics which are indicators of a perceptually nontraditional female role (i.e., well-educated, employed full-time and single) to be positively associated with passage. For the same reason, I expected the fertility rate to be inversely related to adoption. Such characteristics would also seem to indicate that women in some states had already achieved certain public policy goals (i.e., better employment and educational opportunities, greater role options). The passage of the two amendments thus would not be major departures from existing state policies on the status of women.

A related hypothesis was that a state's male-female ratio would be inversely related to passage. Opponents of woman suffrage argued that women were adequately represented in government through their husbands. One concern of opponents of the ERA is that with the amendment the economic role of men will be threatened by the entry of more married women into the labor force. However, in states where there are proportionately more women to men,[15] many women must assume a role other than that of wife and mother. Logically, the legislature should feel an obligation to remove legal barriers and provide direct political representation for such women.

The simple and partial coefficients of correlation between each independent variable and legislative responses to woman suffrage and the ERA are shown in Table 1. As would be expected, the correlates of passage and legislative consensus were quite similar, although the strength of some relationships varied. Since the primary focus here is upon state characteristics associated with passage, only those findings will be fully discussed.

As expected, the legislatures of those states with relatively better educated and more affluent populations were more receptive to passage. Contrary to expectations, however, there was little or no relationship between population, industrialization and adoption. Although the South was a distinctively rural region in 1920, this was not true in the 1970s. Thus, urbanization was related only to suffrage. Conversely, population density was associated only with the ERA, a relationship which reflects the passage of the amendment in all the densely-populated New England and Middle Atlantic states. Although most of the densely-populated Western states also adopted this policy.

Almost all expectations concerning the relationship between political variables and passage were supported. The exception was the linkage found between Democratic control of the state legislature and rejection. Even though each party was in control of comparable numbers of adopting legislatures, a disproportionate number of the laggards were in the Democratic South.

The status of women variables were least helpful in describing legislative responses, perhaps due to the low variability of several measures and to more general problems of measurement.[16] Of five variables, only one was related to all dependent variables, and even here the positive relationship between female educational attainment and passage was weaker than that involving the general population. Only a moderate inverse relationship appeared between the fertility rate and legislative consensus on suffrage, although there were weaker relationships in that direction with other dependent variables.[17] There was a positive relationship between the percentage of single women in the states and ERA passage. And states where men greatly outnumbered

TABLE 1

CORRELATES OF LEGISLATIVE RESPONSES TO ERA AND SUFFRAGE

	Passage				Consensus[a]			
	ERA		Suffrage		ERA		Suffrage	
Variables	R	Partial R[b]	R	Partial R[b]	R	Partial R[b]	R	Partial R[b]
Socioeconomic								
Population	.04	.03	.14	.14	.14	.14	.07	.05
Density	.22	.19	.09	-.01	.30	.28	-.003	-.20
Urbanization	.03	-.12	.28	-.01	.13	.06	.30	-.09
Income	.33	.13	.47	.06	.41	.35	.56	.09
Education	.44	.17	.52	.07	.32	.22	.57	.01
Industrial jobs	-.004	.09	.15	-.13	.07	.11	.11	-.30
Political								
Dem. control	-.48	-.35	-.59	-.12	-.32	-.25	-.60	.07
Competition	.32	.26	.55	.41	.33	.29	.50	.31
Dem. vote	-.39	-.32	-.55	-.17	-.33	-.29	-.64	-.22
Participation	.54	.32	.59	.32	.27	.14	.58	.23
Region (South)	-.49	--	-.67	--	-.24	--	-.78	--
Status of Women								
Single	.35	.21	-.06	-.17	.35	.29	-.16	-.38
Education	.43	.09	.49	.15	.28	.15	.57	.22
Employment	-.15	-.20	-.06	-.26	-.10	-.12	-.08	-.39
Fertility	-.10	-.18	-.20	.11	-.20	-.24	-.32	.01
Sex ratio	.14	.03	.35	.18	.08	.03	.46	.33

All correlations are Pearson R.

[a] Missing from the ERA analysis is Mississippi; missing from the suffrage analysis are Alaska, Hawaii, Vermont, and Florida.

[b] Controlling for Southern regionalism.

women (i.e., the Western states) were most receptive to woman suffrage. A cynic might observe that in such states, women, being a minority, did not pose a political threat to the status quo. On the contrary, Western advocates viewed woman suffrage as crucial to their ideological and partisan goals. Women were perceived as a purifying force in politics. Thus, supporters saw woman suffrage as a means by which the Progressive movement (largely Republican) could succeed in enacting prohibition, immigration restrictions and other neo-Puritanic and traditionalistic policies.[18]

In general, the correlates of passage of the two constitutional amendments are quite similar even though fifty years separate their adoption histories. The strength of the correlations, however, has decreased over time, suggesting that a distinctive inequalitarian political culture, largely regionally-based, may be declining in importance.

As shown in Table 1, when Southern regionalism is controlled, the strong relationships found between the independent variables and legislative responses to the two amendments either disappear or are sharply reduced. Conceptually, regionalism in itself explains nothing. Instead, it is a surrogate measure for a political culture hostile to women's equity issues. When environmental conditions are controlled, the South does not stand out as a peculiarly noninnovative region.[19]

A Model of Policy Innovation on Women's Equity Issues

To further explore the relationship found between political culture and legislative responses to these two issues, I tested a model of policy innovation on women's equity issues using policy outcomes on the ERA only.[20] The model, presented in Figure 1, assumes that a state's propensity to adopt a given policy depends on four factors: the state's historically-based political culture; the state's history of policy making on issues which share some of the intrinsic properties of the policy currently on the agenda; the state's contemporary political environment; and the state's contemporary socioeconomic environment.

The dependent variables here are the two measures of legislative responses to the ERA—direction and consensus—described earlier. Ten independent variables also appear in this model.

Studies indicate that political culture plays a role in shaping patterns of policy making.[21] The concept is also related to several political characteristics of the states.[22] Elazar has described three dominant political cultures: moralistic, individualistic and traditionalistic. Public officials in a moralistic political culture tend to adopt new programs for the good of the communi-

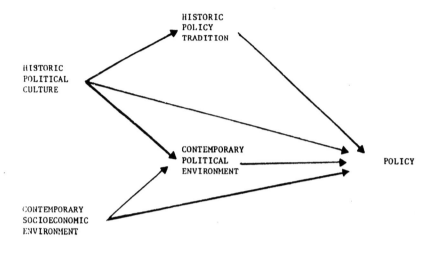

FIGURE 1

A MODEL OF POLICY INNOVATION ON WOMEN'S EQUITY ISSUES

ty. Because of the values of justice and equity stressed by proponents, I expected legislators in states with moralistic cultures to be the most receptive
to the ERA.

Although public officials in an individualistic political culture are normally unwilling to initiate new programs, they will do so when presented
with widespread public demands for such policies. Much evidence of such
demands existed at the time of Congressional passage. The ERA received
overwhelming bipartisan support in both houses of Congress. Heretofore,
the President, most state governors, and several state and federal
bureaucracies endorsed the amendment. A lengthy and impressive list of national associations and interest groups, including, with few exceptions, every
major women's organization, was on record in support of the ERA. Finally, every poll taken on the subject has indicated that a majority of the
American public supports the amendment. Therefore, I expected that the individualistic political culture would be compatible with passage. I recognized,
however, that organized opposition to the amendment, which usually did
not appear until several months after Congressional passage, would present
a more serious threat to passage in responsive individualistic states than in
moralistic states.

The strongest opposition to the ERA should appear in traditionalistic political cultures. Here decision makers accept new policies only if they serve to maintain the status quo or, at most, provide a minimal adjustment to changing conditions. Since the ERA addresses itself to abolishing legal distinctions between men and women, any legislature ratifying the amendment is also committing itself to a program of statutory revision. Although the impact of existing state ERA's does not suggest that sweeping change will follow ratification, the ERA is commonly perceived as a catalyst for social change.[23]

Three measures of a state's policy tradition were: internal unity, innovative tendencies and date of adoption of an equal pay statute. The index of state internal unity is based on the success of each state in resisting national trends in public policy, 1945-1965. This ability derives in part from a high degree of state deviation from national patterns, norms, politics and interests; in part it comes from a high degree of intra-state agreement on these same four areas. Since only 15 of the 50 states had not approved the amendment by 1980, the ERA is a genuine national policy trend. I expected that those states with high internal unity would be most resistant to the ERA.

The state innovative scores reflect patterns of successive policy adoptions in the states, primarily during this century. Although considerable variation occurs in diffusion patterns according to the issue involved and the time-period studied,[24] about half of the states have been rather consistent in their innovative tendencies over time and across issues.[25] Therefore I expected that innovative scores would be positively related to ERA passage.

Finally, I expected that early adoption of an equal pay statute would be positively related to passage. This would support findings that the states are more consistent in being innovative (or noninnovative) on equity policies than on other policy areas.[26]

Per capita personal income served as a measure of affluence. Labor union membership among non-agricultural workers indicated the level of industrialization. Beyond being a measure of industrial economy, labor union membership is also a demand factor in that labor unions have formally endorsed women's equity issues and have attempted to educate their membership on the benefits for all working women. Again, I expected that both variables would be positively related to passage.

Three indicators of mass political behavior used in the comparative study—voting participation, party control of the legislature and party competition—also appear here. It is important, however, that measures of actual demands for public policies be used in determinants research. Studies using measures of membership strength of relevant interest groups on particular issues[27] and measures of state or regional public opinion on agenda items[28] indicate that these preference indicators can be more important determinants of policy outcomes than socioeconomic and other political characteristics. Because of the configuration of public opinion on the ERA,[29] there was no attempt to measure popular support for the ERA. I did include a fourth variable, the combined state membership strength of three major pro-ERA women's organizations—the League of Women Voters, the National Organization for Women and the National Association of Business and Professional Women's Clubs—which I expected to be positively related to passage.

The simple correlations and standardized regression coefficients between the independent variables in the model and legislative responses to the ERA appear in Table 2. As shown by the simple correlations, legislative responses to the ERA are related in the hypothesized direction to all the independent variables.

The multiple regression analysis indicated which of the independent variables are most strongly related to legislative responses to the ERA. A number of moderate relationships appeared between the independent variable and the passage of the ERA. None, however, was of such magnitude to suggest a significantly more parsimonious model. In all, the ten independent variables explain 51 percent of the variance in the passage of the ERA and 35 percent of the variance in legislative consensus on that issue.

The considerable amount of variance left unexplained, particularly in legislative consensus, suggest that one or more variables of general importance may be missing from the model. These could be, among others: public opinion, interest group activity or internal legislative politics. In the case of the ERA, a crucial factor in individual voting decisions was the time period when the amendment first came before the legislature. The addition of a dummy variable (Beta = .43) that indicates whether the state's legislature was in session in 1972 after the date of ERA submission (and before the appearance of a mobilized opposition movement in 1973) raises the explanatory power of the model of legislative consensus to .48.

Although the model should be tested using other women's equity issues from different time periods, the findings here support the basic view that policy outcomes are related both to historical and contemporaneous systemic factors. Women's equity policies, because of the deeply-embedded social values attached to sex roles, may be particularly well-described by a culturally-based innovation-diffusion model.

One problem remains, however: the findings presented here do not explain why woman suffrage became a part of the Consitiution within fifteen months of its submission to the states while the ERA remains three states short of ratification after more than eight years. The findings actually sug-

TABLE 2
ERA AND INDEPENDENT VARIABLES:
CORRELATIONS AND STANDARDIZED REGRESSION COEFFICIENTS

Variables	Passage		Consensus	
	R	Beta[1]	R	Beta[1]
Political Culture				
Traditionalistic	-.61	-.22	-.39	-.23
Policy Tradition				
Internal unity	-.43	-.16	-.47	-.33
Innovation	.41	.26	.40	.20
Equal pay	.34	-.10	.25	-.19
SES Environment				
Income	.33	-.31	.41	-.13
Unionization	.32	.24	.29	.16
Political Environment				
Democratic control	-.48	-.22	-.32	-.04
Competition	.32	.22	.33	.23
Participation	.54	.02	.27	-.08
Group strength	.35	.26	.16	.12
R^2		.51		.35

[1]Missing from the analysis are Alaska, Hawaii, and Mississippi.

gest the opposite; the decline of the South as a distinctively inequalitarian culture should have facilitated passage of the ERA. Further, the pattern of legislative responses to the ERA in the South does not follow Walker's innovation-diffusion model of regional emulation and competition. A majority of the Southern states that did not approve woman suffrage, 1919-1920, made the decision to reject at a time when three or fewer Southern states had passed the measure. On the other hand, seven of the ten Southern states which to date have not approved the ERA made their initial decision to reject after *all* of the six Southern states that have adopted the policy had acted.

At best the findings suggest a set of underlying systemic factors which are compatible with but not sufficient for the adoption of women's equity policies. Needed are more exact issue-specific measures of the contemporary sociopolitical setting as well as some indication of the perceived impact of the policies under consideration.

Despite the similarities between these two women-related constitutional amendments, there are also major differences in their intellectual and political antecedents—differences which are not easily included in any quantitative model. Although the amendments' opponents described the impact of each in broad and very negative terms, the language of the woman suffrage amendment, patterned after the fifteenth amendment, is far more precise. The legal effect of the nineteenth amendment was a major expansion of the electorate. Just as the currently controversial fifth and fourteenth amendments, which guarantee due process and equal protection, are couched in broad language, the ERA, too, contains such latitude. Even ERA proponents acknowledge that not every possible legal consequence can be foreseen prior to ratification. Because of this measure of uncertainty concerning its eventual interpretation by the courts, ERA opponents have been successful in sensationalizing its impact and creating doubts among legislators and the general public. At passage, anti-suffrage arguments concerning the right of each state to establish rules regarding its own electorate had largely eclipsed earlier arguments regarding the demise of home and traditional femininity. Although a states' rights argument against adoption of the ERA is also offered today, the "anti-family" critique of the amendment continues to attract far greater attention and support.

A second key difference between the ratification histories of the two amendments lies in the policy precedents which existed at the time of Congressional passage. Even though the general trend of state and federal policy and court decisions in the area of sex discrimination was consistent with the ERA,[30] only five states had ERA's in their state constitutions before 1972.[31] In contrast, by 1919 fifteen states had granted full voting rights to women and eleven others had extended presidential suffrage to women.[32]

Further, suffragists had a strong central organization at the national level that was instrumental in keeping the state organizations intact. The state woman suffrage associations which in earlier years had waged public education campaigns, contested suffrage referenda and worked for Congressional passage of the federal amendment were poised to press for ratification in 1919. Although in the early years the suffrage movement was plagued by weak state organization and poor financing, these were less serious problems by the time of submission. Those states where strong state associations existed were the first to approve the woman suffrage amendment.[33]

Organizations analogous to the state suffrage associations do not exist to support passage of the ERA in the states. Instead there are over a hundred national groups that formally support the amendment. Of these, less than a dozen have been actively involved in the drive for ratification. Even here, the ERA is only one of several priority issues for these activist multi-purpose groups, and each group has generally pursued separate tactics in working for passage, despite several attempts at coalition formation and coordination of efforts.

Woman suffrage had a further advantage over the ERA in its close alliance with the dominant political movement of that period. At the height of the Progressive era, men and women alike saw woman suffrage as a respectable and legitimate issue, a means of bringing women's natural moral and spiritual concerns to bear upon government. Unlike the new feminist groups most active in working for the ERA today, the suffrage movement was so long-established by 1919 that it too had become conservative and conventional.

Woman suffrage was sent to the states for ratification in June, 1919, after most state legislatures had already adjourned until 1921. The association of suffrage with Progressive middle-of-the-road politics was essential in persuading 30 governors to call special legislative sessions so that the amendment could be ratified in time for women to vote in the 1920 election. The late March, 1972, submission of the ERA also meant that many state legislatures would not be in regular session until 1972. Although 22 states did pass the amendment in 1972, only a handful did so in special session (called for other purposes), and 18 state legislatures did not meet in 1972 after ERA submission. Such a legislative session, however, proved to be the most powerful predictor of legislative support for the ERA, as shown above.

Given the decline of Progressivism in the mid-1920s, it is possible that woman suffrage, like the ERA, could have stalled a few states short of ratificaion had the timing of passage been different. It is undoubtedly true that anti-suffragist forces were less formidable opponents than those working against the ERA. As described by Aileen Kraditor, anti-suffragism was not characterized by mass activity. Although suffrage opponents published several periodicals and organized many societies, their activity was sporadic.[34] The same, however, is generally true of the ERA opposition movement in the first year after Congressional passage.

In conclusion, the empirical research presented here suggests that a somewhat less hostile sociopolitical environment exists for the ERA than for woman suffrage. Even so, several key political differences between the two policies account for the rapid acceptance of woman suffrage in the required 36 states, while the ERA remains three short of the 38 needed for ratification. These differences involve: questions of legal impact, policy precedent, political organization and alliances, the nature of the opposition and the timing of Congressional passage. Given the issue-specific nature of policy formation and the gross measures available for comparative quantitative analysis, such post hoc interpretations are essential for reconciling the perceptual incongruities of policy formation.

NOTES

1. For examples of this type of index see Thomas J. Volgy, "Dimensions of Support for Women's Issues: The Salience of Sexroles," paper presented to the annual meeting of the American Political Science Association, Washington, D.C., 1979; Susan Welch with Diane Levitt Gottheil, "Women and Public Policy: A Comparative Analysis," in *Race, Sex, and Policy Problems* ed. Marian Lief Palley and Michael B. Preston (Lexington, Massachusetts: Lexington , 1979), pp. 193-206.

2. See Robert L. Savage and Diane Kincaid Blair, "Dimensions and Traditions of Responsiveness to Women's Policies in the American States," paper presented at the annual meeting of the Southern Political Science Association, Gatlinburg, 1979 (forthcoming, *Women & Politics*).

3. See Susan B. Hansen, et al., "Women's Political Participation Policy Preferences," *Social Science Quarterly*, 56(March 1976), 576-90; Susan Gluck Mezey, "Attitudinal Consistency Among Political Elites: Implications of Support for the Equal Rights Amendment, "*American Politics Quarterly*, forthcoming; Susan Gluck Mezey and Trudy Haffron Bers, "Support for Women's Issues Among Local Civic Leaders," paper presented at the annual meeting of the American Political Science Association, Washington, D.C., 1979; Savage and Blair, "Dimensions and Traditions"; Susan Welch, "Support Among Women for the Issues of the Women's Movement," *Sociological Quarterly*, 16 (Spring 1975), 216-22.

4. See for example Lawrence E. Gary, "Policy Decisions in the AFDC Program: A Comparative Analysis," *Journal of Politics*, 35 (November 1973), 886-923; Virginia Gray, "Innovation in the States: A Diffusion Study," *American Political Science Review*, 67 (December 1973), 1174-85; Virginia Gray, "Expenditures and Innovation as Dimensions of American States, "*American Journal of Political Science*, 18 (November 1974), 693-99.

5. See Jack L. Walker, "The Deffusion of Innovations among the States," *American Political Science Review*, 63 (September 1969), 880-99.

6. Woman suffrage was first introduced in Congress in 1868 and was sent to the states for ratification in 1919; the equal rights amendment was before Congress, 1923-1972.

7. Only the floor votes on ERA passage appear in the analysis. Since it is the opinion of most legal experts, excepting one Idaho federal judge, that a state cannot rescind its previous approval of a constitutional amendment, votes to rescind may be largely symbolic gestures to appease opponents and influence legislatures that have yet to approve the amendment. In cases of multiple floor votes in a house, I used the most recent vote. In states where only one house of a bicameral legislature has voted on the amendment, that figure represents support in the entire legislature. An assumption of unanimity governs in the case of voice votes. This method of computing consensus results in levels of ERA support above 50% in four states due to the requirement for an extraordinary majority (i.e., by Illinois) or to passage by one house. I excluded states which did not vote on woman suffrage, 1919-1920 and the ERA, 1972-1979, from the analysis of legislative consensus. Again, I considered the passage of the nineteenth amendment after it became a part of the Constitution to be symbolic and ritualistic. For that same reason, I preferred incidence data to speed of adoption of suffrage, 1919-1980.

8. See Robert Eyestone, "Confusion, Diffusion, and Innovation," *American Political Science Review*, 71 (June 1977), 441-47.

9. Walker, "The Diffusion of Innovations."

10. Thomas R. Dye, "Inequity and Civil Rights Policy in the States," *Journal of Politics*, 31 (November 1969), 1080-97.

11. Theodore Lowi, "Toward Functionalism in Political Science: The Case of Innovation in Party Systems," *American Political Science Review*, 57 (September 1963), 580-83; Walker, 'The Diffusion of Innovations."

12. The South, as defined by the Sharkansky typology used here, includes: West Virginia, Kentucky, Tennessee, Texas, Delaware, Maryland, Virginia, North Carolina, South Carolina, Georgia, Florida, Alabama, Mississippi, Arkansas, Louisiana and Oklahoma. Only the first six have approved the suffrage amendment, 1919-1920.

13. See John L. Foster, "Regionalism and Innovation in the American States," *Journal of Politics*, 40 (February 1978), 179-87; Walker, "The Diffusion of Innovations."

14. The employment status of white, married women provides a more precise measure of conformity with traditional sex roles. For a discussion of the discrepancy between traditional sex roles and the economic role of black women, see Mae C. King, "The Politics of Sexual Stereotypes," in *A Portrait of Marginaltiy*, ed. Marianne Githens and Jewel L. Prestage (New York : Longman, 1977), pp.346-65.

15. In most states in 1920 men slightly outnumbered women; the male-female ratio, however, was particularly high in many of the Western states, In 1970, the reverse was true, Women outnumbered men in most states, with only small differences among the states.

16. For a critique of census categories dealing with women see Welch, "Women and Public Policy."

17. For a discussion of the effect of family size on woman suffragism see Richard Jensen, "Family, Career and Reform: Women Leaders of the Progressive Era," in ed. Micheal Gordon *The American Family in Social-Historical Perspective*, (New York: St. Martin's Press, 1973), pp. 267-80.

18. See Alan P. Grimes, *The Puritan Ethic and Woman Suffrage* New York: Oxford University Press, 1967).

19. See Foster, "Regionalism and Innovation." Also, to test for a possible relationship between Southern regionalism and general resistance to amending the U.S. Constitution, I examined the list of adopting states for each of the amendments from the sixteenth (income tax, ratified during the period, 1909-1913) to the proposed twenty-seventh (the ERA). Eight or more states in the region failed to approve five of the twelve amendments. In addition to the two amendments under consideration here, these include: direct election of Senators, District of Columbia electors and abolition of the poll tax—all of which deal with equity as well. The twenty-sixth amendment, lowering the voting age to eighteen, also involves equity. States in the South, as elsewhere, rapidly passed this amendment to avoid establishing two voter registration systems—one for federal elections and one for state and local elections.

20. I deleted suffrage from this analysis because comparable data were not available for several key variables (i.e., an index of internal unity, level of unionization, total memberships in state suffrage organizations and the precedent of a women's equity issue which had gained wide acceptance before Congressional passage of suffrage).

21. Charles A. Johnson, "Political Culture in American States: Elazar's Formulation Examined," *American Journal of Political Science*, 20 (August 1976), 491-509; Ira Sharkansky, "The Utility of Elazar's Political Culture," *Polity*, 2 (Fall 1969), 66-83.

22. Daniel J. Elazar, *American Federalism: A View from the States* (New York: Crowell, 1966); Johnson, "Political Culture."

23. See Barbara A. Brown, et al., *Women's Rights and the Law* (New York: Praeger, 1977); California Commission on the Status of Women, *Impact ERA: Limitations and Possibilities* (Millbrae, California,: Les Femmes, 1976).

24. Gray, "Innovation in the States."

25. Robert L. Savage, "Policy Innovativeness as a Trait of American States," *Journal of Politics*, 40 (February 1978), 212-24.

26. Gray, "Expenditures and Innovation."

27. Ronald Weber and William Shaffer, "Public Opinion and American State Policy-making," *Midwest Journal of Political Science,* 16 (November 1972), 683-99.

28. Robert S. Erikson, "Relationship between Public Opinion and State Policy: A New Look Based on Some Forgotten Data," *American Jounal of Political Science,* 20 (February 1976), 25-36; Anne H. Hopkins, "Opinion Publics and Support for Public Policy in the American States," *American Journal of Political Science,* 18 (February 1974), 167-77; Jeanne Bell Nicholson and Debra W. Stewart, "The Supreme Court, Abortion, and State Response," *Publius,* 8 (Winter 1978), 159-78; Weber and Shaffer, "Public Opinion."

29. See Debrah Bokowski and Aage R. Clausen, "Federalism, Representation, and the Amendment Process: The Case of the Equal Rights Amendment," paper presented at the annual meeting of the Midwest Political Science Association, Chicago, 1979; Joan Huber et al., "Crucible of Opinion on Women's Status: ERA in Illinois," *Social Forces,* 57 (December 1978), 549-65; Mezey and Bers, "Support for Women's Issues." Mezey and Bers found that 98% of a sample of female civic leaders approved of the *language* of the amendment but only 51% supported the "ERA," identified as such. Using 1976 SRC data, Bokowski and Clausen found that despite an approval level of 70% for the ERA, only 21% of the national sample had a position on the issue *and* knew the action taken on it by legislatures in their own states.

30. See Janet K. Boles, *The Politics of the Equal Rights Amendment* (New York: Longman, 1979), pp. 42-45.

31. Seventeen states now have some form of a state ERA and the voters of four additional states—Wisconsin, New York, New Jersey and Florida—rejected such an amendment, 1973-1978.

32. For a list of these states see John J. Stucker, "Women as Voters: Their Maturation as Political Persons in American Society," in *A Portrait of Marginality,* ed. Githens and Prestage, pp. 264-83.

33. See Eleanor Flexner, *Century of Struggle* (New York: Atheneum, 1972), pp. 164-24.

34. Aileen S. Kraditor, *The Ideas of the Woman Suffrage Movement 1980-1920* (Garden City, New York: Anchor, 1971), p. 12.

APPENDIX
LIST OF VARIABLES AND SOURCES[1]

Suffrage-ERA Parallel Analysis

Dependent variables

1. Passage-rejection of ERA.
2. Percent of legislature voting for ERA.
   (Source: newspapers, state legislative reference services.)
3. Passage-rejection of suffrage.
4. Percent of legislature voting for suffrage.
   (Source: World Almanac, 1921, p. 638; The Suffragist.)

Independent variables

Socioeconomic
1. Total population, 1920 and 1970.
2. Population per square mile, 1920 and 1970.
3. Percent urban, 1920 and 1970.
4. Per capita personal income, average, 1919-1921, and 1970.
   (Source: Inter-University Consortium for Political and Social Research.)
5. Percent school attendance by those 7-13 years of age, 1920 and 1970.
6. Percent labor force engaged in manufacturing, 1920 and 1970.

Political
1. Political party in control of the legislature when action taken, 1919-1920, and 1972-1979.
   (Source: The Suffragist, Book of the States.)
2. Index of party competition, 1920-1922, and 1969-1973.
   (Source: ICPSR; Congressional Quarterly Weekly Report.)
   Index is based on two times the percentage of the votes received by the second party in the gubernatorial election in closest proximity to the date when each amendment was submitted to the states for approval.)
3. Percent Democratic vote for Governor, 1920-1922, and 1969-1973.
   (Source: ICPSR; Congressional Quarterly Weekly Report.)
4. Percent turnout, presidential election, 1920 and 1972.
   (Source: ICPSR.)
5. Region (South/non-South).
   (Source: Ira Sharkansky, Regionalism in American Politics, Indianapolis: Bobbs-Merrill, 1969, p. 31.)

Status of Women
1. Percent single women, 14 years and over, 1920 and 1970.[a]
2. Median education of women, 25+, 1970.
3. Percent of female population, 7-20 years, attending school, 1920.
4. Percent white married women in labor force, 1920 and 1970.
5. Fertility rate (children under 5 per 1000 women, 15-49), 1920 and 1970.[b]
6. Number of males per 100 females, 1920 and 1970.

Additional Policy Model Variables

1. Political culture scale.
   (Source: Ira Sharkansky, "The Utility of Elazar's Political Culture," Polity, 2 (Fall 1969), 72.)
2. States' internal unity index.
   (Source: Daniel Elazar, American Federalism: A View from the States, New York: Crowell, 1966, pp. 16-17.)

3. Innovative index.
    (Source: Jack L. Walker, "The Diffusion of Innovations among the
    States," American Political Science Review, 63 (September 1969), 883.)
4. Date of adoption of an equal pay statute, 1919-1974.
    Source: U.S. Women's Bureau, Equal Pay Facts, 1970; compilations
    of state statutes. The first state to adopt the statute in 1919
    received a score of .000 and the last state (in 1974) and non-adopting
    states received a 1.000. All others received a score proportionate to
    year of adoption. See Walker, "Diffusion of Innovations," p. 882.)
5. Labor union membership as a percent of nonagricultural employment, 1970.
6. State members of the League of Women Voters, Business and Professional
    Women's Clubs, and National Organization for Women per 10,000 women,
    18 years and over, in the state's population, 1974.
    (Source: the national offices of each group provided state
    membership figures.)

[1]Unless noted, the source is census data.

[a]1920 data is based on those 15 years and over.

[b]1920 data is based on those 20-40.

WOMEN STATE LEGISLATORS AND THE ERA: DIMENSIONS OF SUPPORT AND OPPOSITION

Joyce R. Lilie
Roger Handberg, Jr.
Wanda Lowrey

ABSTRACT. Attitudes of women state legislators toward ERA are explored in terms of social, institutional-political and cultural correlates. Data base is a mail survey of the 688 women serving in state legislatures in 1977. As a group, women state legislators were heavily in support of ERA. Opposition to ERA is significantly higher among female legislators with lower education, less legislative seniority, who are Republican, from states with legislative party leadership opposed to ERA, in states which elect relatively large percentages of women legislators, and who are from states with moralistic as opposed to traditionalistic political cultures. Group size, psychological and political security, and personal experience of sex discrimination are suggested as explanations.

This study examines the attitudes of one group of women—women state legislators—toward the equal rights amendment. For many, ERA has become the symbol of changing roles for women in modern society. Conflict over ERA ratification is no longer merely a question of defining legal rights and responsibilities. Rather, ERA has taken on a symbolic and highly emotional overlay of conflict over such issues as marriage, divorce, child care, abortion, and homosexuality. As the debate over ERA intensified and became more complex, sharply visible disagreement over ERA also reemerged among women and women's groups.

Historically, the women's movement in the U.S. has been marked by strong divisions among women themselves over political goals and strategies and more generally over appropriate roles for women in society. The split in the 1870s between the National Woman Suffrage Association and the American Woman Suffrage Association is an early example, and in the 1880s and 1890s several organizations opposed to women's suffrage were led by women.[1] In 1923, when the ERA was first introduced in Congress, the

Joyce R. Lilie is an Associate Professor of Political Science at Florida International University, Miami, FL 33199. Roger Handberg, Jr., is a Professor of Political Science, affiliated with the University of Central Florida, Orlando, FL 32816. Wanda Lowrey is with the department of Political Science at the University of Central Florida, Orlando, FL 32816.

23

Woman's Party supported it, but organizations concerned with the amendment's impact on protective labor legislation opposed it. As late as 1968, several prominent national women's groups opposed the ERA.[2]

After the ERA was approved by Congress in 1972, the amendment moved through rapid, low-conflict ratification in 28 states, where state legislators apparently perceived little or no organized opposition to ERA.[3] By late 1973, conflict over ratification intensified. Seven additional states ratified the amendment only after sharp conflict in their legislatures. Rescission efforts have been undertaken in 14 states, and have passed in four. Conflict remains intense in the extension period, with ultimate ratification of the amendment in serious doubt. As debate over ERA has intensified, organized opposition to the amendment has included several highly visible individual women and *ad hoc* women's groups.[4] The pattern of women opposing women, often cited as an important characteristic differentiating women from other minority groups,[5] has continued through the 1970s in the struggle over the equal rights amendment. Given this history of women opposing women, it is important to delineate the dimensions of support and opposition among women state legislators regarding ERA.

Women state legislators were selected for study in part because they have been or will be participating in the ratification process and in part because of the likely importance of the attitudes of female decision makers on issues relating to women. Women are not likely to occupy key legislative positions[6] nor are their numbers as legislators large. It is, however, likely that female legislators serve as positive or negative cue givers for their male colleagues on issues that are perceived as having particular relevance to women. Several studies have identified the importance of cue giving and cue taking in legislative decision making.[7] The impact of opposition to ERA by female legislators is magnified if it is used by uncertain or opposing male legislators to legitimize negative votes.

Existing studies suggest that women state legislators generally support ERA. A 1977 survey of women elites conducted by the Center for American Women in Politics found that a large percentage of female legislators support ERA, and that female office holders in general were more supportive of the amendment than their male counterparts.[8] Using recorded legislative votes, Shelah Leader found that women legislators were more likely than men to vote for ERA, in both ratified and unratified states, but that party also influenced vote on ERA, resulting in no appreciable difference in support levels between Democratic men and Republican women.[9] However, studies of other female activists, and of other women's issues, show highly mixed patterns of support and opposition among women. Susan Mezey has concluded that women politicians are influenced by their political environment and institutional setting to emphasize their role as politicians more than their role as defenders of women's rights.[10]

Previous research also suggests that opposition to ERA is greater among women legislators who are older, less educated and less liberal. Kent Tedin, et al., identified these differences among ERA activists in Texas,[11] and Theodore Arrington and Patricia Kyle found that North Carolina anti-ERA women were less well educated, likely to be housewives, and more likely to be married to men in lower status occupations than were pro-ERA activist women.[12] These studies are not entirely comparable to the present research since the former analyzes issue activists, not legislators, and draw their samples from a single state. However, their findings compare with the conventional wisdom that opposition to ERA is strongest among the socially and politically conservative, older, more traditional segments of society which most fear the changing sex roles and social relationships which the amendment symbolizes. We also expected that opposition to ERA would be strongest among Republicans, since opposition to ERA is viewed as a conservative position, and among Southerners, since most of the states which have not ratified ERA are Southern. We further hypothesized that ERA opposition would be highest in states with a traditionalistic political culture, since that political culture emphasizes status, authority and conservation of existing social relationships.

Characteristics of the Sample

The data for this study consist of the responses to a 1977 mail survey of the 688 women who then served in state legislatures. The return rate was 61%, producing 418 usable questionnaires. Responses were obtained from 47 states.[13] Senators were overrepresented in the sample return (71%, N = 73), while representatives were slightly underrepresented (57%, N = 333). Two replies were from unicameral Nebraska, while 10 replies could not be classified as to state. Democrats, Republicans and independents were represented in the sample in almost exactly the proportion they exist in the population. The characteristics of women in our sample are summarized in Table 1.

For nearly 43% of our sample, no vote had been taken on ERA while the legislators were in office. In order to include this group of women within our study, we measured attitude toward ERA and used attitude, rather than vote, as a dependent variable.

Table I
Women State Legislators 1977

A. Party Identification

	Democratic	Republican	Independent	NR
Entire Sample	61.7%	34.7%	1.2%	2.4%
N	(258)	(145)	(5)	(10)
Excluding N.H.	65.1%	31.6%	1.4%	1.9%
N	(235)	(114)	(5)	(7)

B. Education

	Less than Highschool	Highschool	Some College	College Grad.	College Plus	NR
Entire Sample	.5%	7.4%	22.5%	23.5%	44.0%	2.6
N	(1)	(31)	(94)	(98)	(183)	(11)
Excluding N.H.	0	6.6%	22.2%	22.7%	46.3%	2.2%
N	0	(24)	(80)	(82)	(167)	(8)

C. Age

	21-39	40-49	50-59	60-69	70+	NR
Entire Sample	23.2%	28.2%	28.9%	11.0%	1.4%	6.5%
N	(97)	(118)	(121)	(46)	(6)	(27)
Excluding N.H.	22.7%	29.0%	29.9%	11.4%	.2%	6.6%
N	(82)	(105)	(108)	(41)	(1)	(24)

D. Occupation

	House-wife	Blue Collar	White Collar	Self Employed	Volun-teer	Student	NR
Entire Sample	28.2%	1.4%	58.8%	2.6%	3.1%	2.2%	3.6%
N	(117)	(6)	(244)	(11)	(13)	(9)	(15)
Excluding N.H.	28.2%	1.1%	59.6%	2.8%	3.6%	1.9%	3.0%
N	(101)	(4)	(215)	(10)	(13)	(7)	(11)

E. Length of Service in Legislature

	0-2 Years	3-4 Years	More than 4 Years	NR
Entire Sample	34.9%	25.5%	36.3%	2.6%
N	(146)	(107)	(152)	(11)
Excluding N.H.	34.1%	27.7%	37.2%	1.0%
N	(123)	(100)	(138)	(5)

Findings

As a group, women state legislators were heavily in support of ERA. Seventy-two % (N = 301) indicated support of ERA while 12.2% (N = 51) opposed it. Two % said they were unconcerned with ERA; 13.8% (N

= 58) did not report a position on the amendment.[14] The small number of identifiable opponents limits the analysis. Several hypotheses cannot be tested because the sample size is attenuated when controls are introduced. Three categories of variables are associated with opposition to ERA: social attributes, institutional-political setting and state political culture. Generally, female legislators with lower education level, with less legislative seniority, who are Republican, who are from states with legislative party leadership opposed to ERA, who are from states which elected relatively large percentages of women to their legislature, and those who are from states with moralistic as opposed to traditionalistic political cultures are more likely to oppose ERA. A number of these relationships are the reverse of that which was expected and therefore require careful explanation. It is also likely that these variables interact in complex ways which we can suggest rather than test, given the small number of ERA opponents.

We said earlier that we expected to find a "generation gap" on ERA. Age has consistently been found to be one of the strongest correlates of support for women's rights.[15] Younger women, who have been more exposed to ideas and experiences at odds with traditional women's roles, and have obtained more education and entered the work force (or accepted the idea that they will do so), have presumably thereby come to be more aware of sexual discrimination, to reject traditional sex roles and to be more supportive of women's rights. We therefore hypothesized that among women state legislators, support for ERA would decrease with increased age. As Table 2-A shows, however, the relationship between age and support for ERA is not a significant one. Older women legislators are nearly as likely as their younger colleagues to support ERA.

To further probe the impact of age, we tested the relationship between length of service in the legislature and support for ERA, reasoning that there might be a "generation gap" defined in terms of years of legislative service rather than in terms of chronological age. These findings are reported in Table 2-B. Here the relationship is signficant, but in the opposite direction—women who have served more than four years in the legislature are significantly more likely to *support* ERA and *less* likely to oppose it than those who have been in the legislature two years or less.

This relationship does not rest on education—the less senior women do not significantly differ from the more senior in level of education. The less senior are younger; this is reflected in the declining age of women state legislators as a group. The explanation could possibly be electoral; but it would be a strange combination of electoral dynamics which at one and the same time had defeated senior anti-ERA legislators while producing new

Table II

Social Correlates of ERA Attitudes

A. Age

	Under 40	40-49	50-59	60 and over
Legislator's ERA Views				
Favor	91.0%	90.0%	83.3%	82.4%
Oppose	9.0%	10.0%	16.3%	17.6%
N	(78)	(100)	(102)	(51)

x^2=4.102, n.s., gamma=.235

B. Length of Service In Legislature

	0-2 Years	3-4 Years	Over 4 Years
Legislator's ERA Views			
Favor	60.3%	74.8%	80.9%
Oppose	17.8%	2.8%	13.6%
DK/NR	21.9%	22.4%	5.6%
N	(146)	(107)	(162)

x^2=33.680, p=.000, gamma=-.337

C. Occupation

	House-wife	Blue Collar	White Collar	Self Employed	Volunteer	Student
Legislator's ERA Views						
Favor	80.2%	75.0%	87.3%	81.8%	100%	100%
Oppose	19.8%	25.0%	12.7%	18.2%	0	0
N	(117)	(6)	(244)	(11)	(13)	(9)

x^2=6.750, n.s., Cramer's V=-.141

D. Education

	High School	Some College	College Grad	College Plus
Legislator's ERA Views				
Favor	59.3%	78.5%	92.4%	90.0%
Oppose	40.7%	21.5%	7.6%	10.0%
N	(27)	(79)	(79)	(160)

x^2=23.797, p.000, gamma=-.414

women legislators who oppose ERA. The explanation which we find most persuasive is that more senior legislators have had more personal, professional and political experience of sexual discrimination than their more junior colleagues, for whom the path had already been *relatively* cleared of sexual bias. This greater experience of discrimination increases salience of ERA. At the same time, longer experience in politics, safer electoral position and the greater power within legislatures which comes with seniority make it less risky to support ERA. Psychologically, greater experience may increase self-confidence and sense of personal efficacy, making it easier to reject traditional sex roles. The less senior find the issue of ERA less salient, and without electoral safety or the protection of seniority, find it more difficult to support ERA. This explanation seems plausible; personal interviews would be necessary to establish whether it is accurate. Whatever the explanation, there is no "generation gap" regarding ERA among women legislators when the measure of generation is chronological age, but there is a kind of "reverse generation gap" when the measure is length of service in the legislature.

Occupation does not distinguish ERA opponents from proponents. For this reason, Table 2-C gives a more detailed breakdown than might usually be presented, especially given the small numbers in several categories. Given the elite nature of the sample, this pattern fits the notion that ERA support increased with general social and economic position.

ERA support is clearly related to educational level of the legislator. As educational level advances, support for ERA increases (Table 2-D). All groups are supportive—the more educated simply grow more supportive. This is consistent with most analysis which finds education an important determinant of pro-women's rights attitudes. Further, education has been associated with increased civic competence and civic activity levels. Education may be particularly important in giving women confidence in asserting their legislative positions. Irene Diamond reported several instances in which women legislators took unobtrusive legislative postures in part because of feelings of personal inadequacy. Education may have helped overcome these inhibitions. Overcoming the psychological barriers then contributes to support for ERA and the new world symbolized by the amendment. Again, personal interviews would be necessary to establish whether these linkages actually exist.

Three institutional-political variables are significantly related to women legislators' position on ERA. Support and opposition are related to party affiliation, to perception of the position taken by legislative party leadership, and to whether the state had ratified ERA. Nationally, both Democratic and Republican presidents and party platforms (up to 1980) supported ERA, although on the whole national Democratic leaders have been more overtly supportive. One would not necessarily expect the bipartisan support of national leaders to be reflected in the state legislatures, however. Clearly there is great variation among the states in the extent to which party influences legislative voting decisions; party is more influential in competitive two party states, and is especially important on issues of social and economic policy.[16] Leader found that party was an important determinant of state legislative votes on ERA for both men and women.[17] Our data substantiate that finding for women. As Table 3-A shows, a majority of women in both parties support ERA, but opponents are disproportionately Republican. The percentage of Republicans who oppose ERA is almost five times that of opposing Democrats. ERA has taken on strong ideological coloration, being linked to conservative positions on states rights, abortion, the drafting of women and other issues. A number of conservative groups, e.g., The John Birch Society, have actively opposed ERA. Several studies show that opposition to women's issues is associated with conservative positions on other issues. These factors undoubtedly help account for the disproportionately Republican opposition to ERA, but there is also an interaction with education here, since the education level of Democratic women legislators is somewhat higher than that of Republicans.

Women state legislators are significantly more likely to oppose ERA when they perceive that their legislative party leadership opposes the amendment and to support ERA when they see their leadership as supportive (Table 3-B). This may indicate that women legislators are responsive to party leaders on ERA. Or, it may indicate that women legislators see ERA as part of a more general partisan environment, related through party leadership to other legislative issues, including their own power positions and ability to be successful on other questions. It may also be that the electoral factors and general political setting which produced leadership opposition also produced opposition among women legislators. While a majority of party leaders are perceived as supporting ERA, opposed party leadership is concentrated in states which have not yet ratified the amendment, magnifying the political importance of the tie between the position taken by female legislators and their party leaders.

The third factor related to women legislators' attitudes toward ERA is whether the state in which a woman serves has ratified the amendment. As shown in Table 3-C, the pattern is clear. Nonratified states have larger proportions of both supporting and opposing women legislators than ratified states do. In ratified states, 20% said they were unconcerned with ERA, didn't know their position on ERA, or did not respond to the question. In ratified states, women legislators apparently view the issue as settled or unimportant or at least as one on which it is unnecessary to take a stand. It is less easy to be noncommittal in unratified states, where only 4% said they were unconcerned or reported no position. In these states, ERA is more

Table III

Institutional - Political Correlates of ERA Attitudes

A. Political Party

	Democrat	Republican	Independent
Legislator's ERA Views			
Support	93.2%	73.5%	100%
Oppose	6.8%	33.3%	0
N	(220)	(117)	(5)

x^2 = 26.194, p= .000, Cramer's V = .227

B. Party Leadership Position

	Leadership Supports	Leadership Opposes	Leadership Split
Legislator's ERA Views			
Support	87.0%	55.8%	90.7%
Oppose	7.0%	30.2%	4.7%
DK/NR	6.0%	14.0%	4.7%
N	(285)	(43)	(43)

x^2 = 30.990, p = .000, Cramer's V = .204

C. Has State Ratified ?

	State Has Ratified	State Has Not Ratified
Legislator's ERA Views		
Support	69.9%	78.6%
Oppose	10.6%	17.5%
DK/NR	19.6%	3.9%
N	(312)	(100)

x^2 = 15.961, p = .000, Cramer's V = .196

salient, the level of conflict higher, and the pressure to take a position is undoubtedly greater. Media coverage, organized group activity and election campaigns increase pressure on legislators to take positions on ERA in unratified states.

Since 11 of the 15 states which have not ratified ERA are Southern or border states, one might predict that women state legislators' support for ERA would show a regional pattern. As Table 4-A shows, this is not the case when

Table IV

Regional and Cultural Correlates of ERA Attitudes

A. Region

	Northeast	South	Southwest/West	Midwest	North-west	Pacific
Legislator's ERA Views						
Favor	87.5%	88.4%	81.5%	83.5%	84.2%	100%
Oppose	12.5%	11.6%	18.5%	16.5%	15.8%	0.0
N	(104)	(69)	(27)	(103)	(38)	(7)

x^2 = 2.746, n.s., Cramer's V = .277

B. Political Culture

	Moralistic	Individualistic	Traditionalistic
Legislator's ERA Views			
Favor	68%	75%	78%
Oppose	14%	8%	15%
DK/NR	18%	17%	7%
N	(190)	(130)	(81)

x^2 = 7.789, p = .009, Cramer's V = 160

C. Percentage Women In Legislature

	0-9.9% Women	10-19.9% Women	20% + Women
Legislator's ERA Views			
Support	73%	70%	63%
Oppose	10%	14%	11%
DK/NR	16%	15%	26%
N	(180)	(151)	(73)

x^2 = 27.074, p = .007, gamma = .195

one uses census designations of region. Women legislators in all regions support ERA, showing higher levels of support and lower levels of opposition in the Southern and Pacific states, but the relationship is not significant. Nonetheless, the direction of differences in Table 4-A is interesting. Failure of southern states to ratify ERA rests on opposition from male, not female legislators.

There is, however, reason to believe that census-type classifications obscure rather than clarify regularities and differences among the states. Daniel Elazar and others[19] have developed the concept of political culture as a basis for classifying states. Political culture—"the particular pattern or orientation to political action in which each state is embedded"—rests on shared values and traditions more than on geography. As Norman Luttbeg says, political culture reflects "ideational elements passed from one generation to the next"[20] embodying shared traditions, values, social biases, life styles, resources and problems. Political culture has been shown to be a useful concept for explaining differences among the states. For example, Luttbeg found a cultural classification more useful than classifications based on geography, economic development or political competition for explaining policy outputs in such areas as welfare and education, while Ira Sharkansky demonstrated state differences tied to culture, independent of economic development or urbanism.[21]

Elazar identified three principal political cultures in the U.S.— individualistic, moralistic and traditionalistic. Individualistic political culture views the political order as a nonideological market place in which government's role is to provide services demanded by the people, not to define the public good nor to intervene in private affairs beyond the minimum necessary to keep order. A moralistic political culture stresses positive government action in the communal interest, regulation of economic and social life, and politics as a "means of coming to grips with the issues and public concerns of our society."[22] Traditionalistic culture has a more paternalistic and elitist conception of the political order, emphasizing authority, hierarchy and politics as a conserving and custodial process for society.[23]

We hypothesized that women legislators' support for ERA would be highest in states with moralistic political cultures, because that culture puts relatively greater emphasis on government action to ensure rights and on government intervention in the private sphere. We expected support to be lowest in traditionalistic states with their emphasis on status, hierarchy and maintenance of the existing social order. In fact, as Table 4 indicates, the relationship is the reverse. A larger percentage of women legislators support ERA in traditionalistic political cultures than in moralistic cultures. Women in traditionalistic states are also less likely to be unconcerned or noncommittal (7% vs. 18%). Whatever may be the patterns of mass opinion in the categories of states, and whatever pattern may hold among male legislators or other elites, women state legislators are more likely to support ERA in traditionalist states. [24]

One part of the explanation for this relationship is found in the fact that of the 15 states which have not ratified ERA, 11 fall into the traditionalistic category while only one (Utah) is a moralistic state. The fact of nonratification increases support among women state legislators. It may be that the same culture which produces a political climate which makes ratification of ERA difficult also produces women legislators who support the amendment, although nonratification in and of itself very probably has an independent effect.

Further, as shown by Table 4-C, women are significantly more likely to support ERA in states with *low* percentages of women in the legislature than in states with a relatively *large* proportion of women in State House or Senate. (82% support in the states with less than 5% women legislators; 56% support in states with more than 25% women legislators.) Diamond has argued that a moralistic political culture is a necessary but not sufficient condition for the election of larger proportions of women and that traditionalistic political cultures elect fewer women.[25] Thus, if one views political culture as the basic explanatory variable, the line of argument is as follows. A moralistic culture, stressing government intervention in the private sphere, helps create the conditions for electing women and for ratification of ERA, and at the same time produces circumstances in which women legislators are free to oppose or be indifferent to ERA. We know from Diamond's work that state legislatures with large percentages of women are also likely to contain "housewife bench warmers," whose role concepts make them feel incapable of dealing with legislative issues, and further, to contain "traditional civic workers," whose values are not particularly oriented towards women's issues.[26] The presence of these categories of women helps account for the relatively large percentage of unconcerned women from states with larger female delegations. The fact that these states are likely to have ratified ERA further reduces the salience of the issue. On the other hand, traditionalistic political cultures have neither elected large percentages of women to the legislature nor ratified ERA. The lack of ratification increases the salience of ERA, making it more important for women legislators to take a position on the amendment. At the same time a reactive response, perhaps even a "besieged mentality" may develop among the relatively small numbers of women in traditional state legislatures, thus increasing support for ERA. Both Mezey and Rosabeth Kanter argue that when women operate as a very small minority, especially where women are not "generally" accepted, they are likely to develop greater sex-role awareness, and to be more aware of discrimination. This may be part of the dynamic of interaction among political culture, percentage of women in state legislatures, ratification of ERA, and women state legislators' support or opposition toward ERA.

Conclusions

While a large percentage of women state legislators support ratificatioii of the equal rights amendment, an identifiable minority oppose ratification. On many legislative issues, 12% opposition would be considered insignificant. For 12% of women legislators to oppose an amendment understood to advance women's legal rights is, in comparative perspective, significant. If the group involved were blacks, not women, 12% opposition would be a remarkable finding. The history of women opposing women on women-related issues is reflected in and repeated by this group of visible women elites involved, directly and symbolically, in conflict over a highly controversial issue of public policy affecting women. Our findings, however, do not support the conclusion that failure to ratify ERA rests with women state legislators. To the contrary, levels of support for the amendment are higher among women in unratified than in ratified states. Particularly in the Southern states, our findings indicate that the fate of ERA rests in the hands of male, not female, legislators.

Our findings point to a number of tactical suggestions for proponents of ERA. First, there are relatively few uncommitted female legislators in the unratified states. Secondly, the link between female legislators' attitudes toward ERA and their perceptions of their party leadership's position on the amendment, along with the concentration of opposed leadership in the unratified states, suggests that focusing on party leadership might be a fruitful strategy for improving the chances of ratification. Finally, since junior legislators are less supportive of ERA than their senior colleagues, the election of larger number of women to state legislatures in and of itself is unlikely in the short run to increase legislative support for ERA. In the longer run, as newly-elected female legislators accumulate seniority, the association of seniority with support for ERA may have the effect of increasing support for the amendment. In the process of ERA ratification, however, the longer run will be irrelevant.

Our study throws some light on the interaction of role concept with seniority in the explanation of legislative decision making. Mezey and others have concluded that one reason why women in positions of political power are not more likely to support feminist issues is that the socialization process for such women emphasizes the ''politician'' role rather than the role of ''defender of women's issues.'' We suggest a modification of that conclusion. For women state legislators, at least, institutional position and role conception appear to interact, with junior legislators more likely to adopt the "politician" role, accepting such norms as bargaining and compromise. The more senior women, with more insitiutional, personal and political resources, are more likely to reject the "politician" for the "feminist" role and thus, in this case, to support ERA.

· This study also lends some support for the use of political culture to explain public policy differences among the states. Classification of states, based on political culture, related to support and opposition for ERA, while merely regional classification did not. We show that states with traditionalistic cultures have neither elected many women to their legislatures nor ratified ERA and thus have created twin circumstances encouraging female legislators to support ERA.

We have identified the general dimensions of support and opposition regarding ERA among women state legislators, but are limited by our research instrument, a mail survey. As Leader has pointed out, ERA is viewed by most feminists as the "bedrock pro-woman issue" and as a benchmark by which legislators can be evaluated. For this reason if no other, it is important to gain greater understanding of the attitudes of women state legislators toward ERA. However, the patterns of support and opposition for ERA may be quite different than those for other women's issues. As a consititutional amendment and as an issue which has become the focus for much controversy about changing sex roles, ERA may elicit quite different patterns than more narrowly-drawn legislative issues. Robert Savage and Diane Blair have demonstrated that women's public policy issues are multidimensional and that these issues have historically elicited multidimensional responses from state legislatures. Comparing the patterns identified here with patterns of legislators' attitudes toward other women's issues would be a useful next research step.

FOOTNOTES

1. William L. O'Neill, *Everyone Was Brave* (Chicago: Quadrangle Books, 1971).

2. Janet K. Boles, *The Politics of the Equal Rights Amendment* (New York: Longman, 1979), pp. 41-42.

3. *Ibid.*, pp 61-84.

4. *Ibid.*, pp 101-40.

5. William H Chafe,*Women and Equality* (London: Oxford University Press, 1977), pp.56-57.

6. Irene Diamond, *Sex Roles in the State House* (New Haven, Connecticut: Yale University Press, 1977), pp. 156-69.

7. Raymond Bauer, Ithiel do Sola Pool and Lewis Anthony Dexter, *American Business and Public Policy* (New York: Aldine, 1963, 1972);John W. Kingdon, *Congressmen's Voting Decisions* (New York: Harper, Row 1973), pp. 69-104; and Donald R. Matthews and James A Stimson, *Yeas and Nays: Normal Decision-Making in the U.S. House of Representatives* (New York: Wiley, 1975).

8. Rutgers University, Center for the American Woman in Politics, *Women in Public Office* (R.R. Bowaker, 1977), p. 1a.

9. Shelah Gilbert Leader, "The Policy Impact of Elected Women Officials," in *The Impact of the Electoral Process*, ed. Louis Maisel and Joseph Cooper, (Beverly Hills: Sage, 1977), 265-84.

10. Susan Gluck Mezey, "Support For Women's Rights Policy," *American Politics Quarterly*, 6 (October 1978), 485-97. Also see Frieda L Gehlen, "Women Members of Congress: A Distinctive Role," in *A Portrait of Marginality* ed. Marianne Githens and Jewel Prestage (New York: McKay, 1977), pp.304-19; John W. Soule and Wilma E. McGrath, "A Comparative Study of Male-Female Political Attitudes at Citizen and Elite Levels," in Githens and Prestage, *Portrait of Marginality*, pp. 196-209; Jessie Bernard, "Age, Sex and Feminism," *Annals of the American Academy of Political and Social Sciences*, 415 (September 1974); Susan Hansen, "Women's Political Participation and Policy Preferences," *Social Science Quarterly*, 56 (March 1976), 578; Susan Welch, "Support Among Women for the Issues of the Women's Movement," *The Sociological Quarterly*, 16 (Spring 1975), 216-27; Virginia Sapiro, "News From the Front: Inter-sex and Inter-generational Conflict Over the Status of Women," paper presented at the annual meeting of the American Political Science Association, Washington, D.C., 1977.

11. Kent L. Tedin, et al., "Social Background and Political Differences Among Pro-and Anti-ERA Activists,"*American Politics Quarterly*, 5 (July 1977), 395-408.

12. Theodore S. Arrington and Patricia A. Kyle, "Equal Rights Amendment Activists in North Carolina," paper presented to the annual meeting of the American Political Science Association, San Francisco, 1975.

13. Low rates of return were obtained from California, Kentucky, Maine, New Jersey and Texas. A national sample of women state legislators must allow for the fact that a disproportionate number of women are elected to the large, citizen legislature in New Hampshire, and that those women may differ significantly from women state legislators nationally. 12.9% of our sample is from New Hampshire. Table I presents a summary of the characteristics of our sample when those from New Hampshire are excluded. As can be seen in Table I, the presence or absence of women from New Hampshire does not substantially alter the sample. New Hampshire women were more Republican than the national sample, and slightly more likely to oppose ERA (14.8% vs. 12.2%). They were less educated than the national sample in the sense that fewer had degrees beyond college but more educated in the sense that a larger percentage in New Hampshire had completed college. Occupationally, New Hampshire has sightly more housewives, students and blue collar workers but a lower proportion of volunteers than the national sample. New Hampshire has a greater percentage of women who have been in the legislature 2 years or less, but also has a greater percentage of women with 4 or more years service than does the national sample. In sum, New Hampshire's female legislators were somewhat different than the national sample in 1977, but their differences and their numbers combined were not great enough to alter the results of our analysis.

14. We also asked about vote; among the 57% of the sample who had voted on ERA, 82% said they voted for the amendment, 17% said they voted against it.

15. Welch, "Support Among Women," p. 222; Sapiro, "News from the Front," p. 17.

16. Glen T. Broach, "A Comparative Dimensional Analysis of Parties and Urban-Rural Voting In State Legislatures," *Journal of Politics*, (August 1972), 905-921; Hugh LeBlanc, "Voting In State Senates," *Midwest Journal of Political Science*, (February 1967) 27-57.

17. Leaper "Policy Impact."

18. Arrington and Kyle, "ERA Activists," p.4; Welch "Support Among Voters," p. 224.

19. Daniel Elazar, *American Federalism: A View From the States* (New York: Crowell, 1972) especially pp. 79-116. Among many others see Samuel C. Patterson, "The Political Cultures of the American States," *Journal of Politics*,[30] (February 1968), 187-209; Ira Sharkansky, "The Utility of Elazar's Political Culture: A Research Note," *Polity*,[2] (Fall 1969), 66-85; Robert L. Savage, "Patterns of Multilinear Evolution in the American States,"*Publius*,[3] (Spring 1973), 75-108; Norman R. Luttbeg, "Classifying the American States: An Empirical Attempt

to Identify Internal Variation," *Midwest Journal of Political Science*,[15] (November 1971), 703-21.

20. Luttbeg. "Classifying American States," p. 705.

21. *Ibid.*; Sharkansky, "Utility of Elazar's Political Culture."

22. Elazar, *American Federalism*, p. 91.

23. We follow Elazar in classifying the states, as follows:
   —Moralistic: Vermont, Minnesota, Utah, Maine, Michigan, Wisconsin, North Dakota, Colorado, Oregon, New Hampshire, Iowa, Kansas, California, Washington, Montana, South Dakota, Idaho.
   —Individualistic: Connecticut, Nebraska, Wyoming, Massachusetts, Rhode Island, New York, Pennsylvania. New Jersey, Ohio, Illinois, Indiana, Nevada, Delaware, Maryland, Missouri.
   —Traditionalistic: Texas, Oklahoma, West Virginia, Kentucky, Florida, Alabama, Georgia, Arkansas, Louisiana, Virginia, South Carolina, Mississippi, North Carolina, Tennessee, Arizona and New Mexico.
Analysis was also performed using Elazar's eight categories which indicate combinations of different strains of political culture within states, but these finer distinctions did not change the analysis.

24. Using different classifications of the states produced comparable results. For example, using Robert L. Savage's classification of states showed the highest levels of support for ERA to be among women legislators in Southern states (85.5%), intermediate levels in Industrial (75.5%) and Frontier (69.5%) states, and the lowest in Southwestern (58.1%). Savage suggests that the Southern states are most nearly comparable to Elazar's Traditionalistic states, Industrial to Individualistic and Frontier to Moralistic. Thus the basic direction of differences is the same, using the Savage classification, as the Elazar classification. Robert L. Savage, "Patterns of Multilinear Evolution in the American States," *Publius*, (Spring 1973), pp. 75-108. Using Norman Luttbeg's classification produces similar results, although in neither case did the relationships quite reach acceptable significance levels. Luttbeg, "Classifying the American States."

25. Diamond, *Sex Roles*, pp. 21-24.

26. *Ibid.*, pp. 162-64.

27. Mezey, "Support for Women's Rights Policy," p. 22; Rosabeth Moss Kanter, "Some Effects of Proportions on Group Life: Skewed Sex Ratios and Responses to Token Women" *American Journal of Sociology*, 82 (March 1977), 965-90.

28. Robert L. Savage and Diane Kincaid Blair, "Dimensions and Traditions of Responsiveness to Women's Policies in the American States," paper presented to the annual meeting of the Southern Political Science Association, Gatlinburg, Tennessee, 1979, forthcoming, *Women & Politics*.

POLITICAL IDEOLOGY
OF PRO- AND ANTI-ERA WOMEN

Iva E. Deutchman
Sandra Prince-Embury

ABSTRACT. This study explored political ideology, religiosity and attitudes toward women among six pro-ERA and six anti-ERA women, all of whom are politically active. In-depth interviews were used to assess multi-dimensionality of political ideology in our sample. Standardized inventories were used to assess religiosity and attitudes toward women. Predicted differences were found between pro- and anti-ERA women in this sample in religiosity as well as attitudes toward women. In-depth interview techniques allowed a comparative analysis of political ideologies in these two groups which confirmed broad-based ideological differences.

Introduction

The proposed twenty-seventh amendment to the U.S. Constitution, known as the equal rights amendment (ERA), has become the source of controversy between two opposing forces of politically active women. This study examines two small samples of highly and equally active ERA proponents and opponents in order to elucidate ideological underpinnings of ERA preference. We hypothesized that ERA preference was undoubtedly linked to overall political ideology. Through the use of in-depth interviews we were able to explore the multifaceted nature of political ideology, and its relationship to ERA preference.

ERA activists on either side of the issue have only recently come to the attention of scholars as appropriate subjects for study. David Brady and Kent Tedin[1] have suggested that differences in religious orthodoxy and church attendance largely account for the political ideology of anti-ERA women. Subsequent research by Tedin[2] and Tedin et al.[3], has substantiated religious

Iva E. Deutchman is with Women and Power Institute, University of Pennsylvania. Dr. Sandra Prince-Embury is an Assistant Professor of Psychology, Pennsylvania State University, Capitol Campus #10, Middletown, PA 17057. The authors would like to thank Frederick Frey and Sarah Slavin for their helpful suggestions in reviewing our manuscript.

differences between the pro and the anti female activists, as well as differences between pro- and anti-ERA women in income and education, although these latter differences were not postulated to be as significant as religiosity.

This study expands upon the aforementioned research by examining, through in-depth interviewing, not only demographic and religious variables but also activists' attitudes toward women and broader-based political ideology. The in-depth interviews allowed each respondent to discuss perceived consequences of ERA ratification or defeat, a useful analytic approach because previous research has not dealt with the ideological complexity of ERA preference, using instead standard political ideology scales which often ignore the multi-dimensional nature of ideology. In-depth interviewing allows the researcher to obtain a great deal of information, in a way that is flexible and adaptable to the individual situation.[4]

Method

Volunteers were recruited from major women's organizations, in Pennsylvania, Virginia and Maryland, which were actively working for either ERA passage or defeat. These organizations include Stop ERA and Eagle Forum (opposed), National Organization for Women (several chapters) and ERAmerica (favorable). Members from these cooperating organizations who were willing to participate in the study were contacted and interviewed from one to two hours each at their homes. Interviews were taped for later content analysis.

It should be noted that not all respondents were themselves members of the contacted organizations, although majorities in both cases were. One of the anti-ERA women, a member of Conservative Caucus, was well known to a state coordinator of Stop ERA, who suggested this woman be interviewed. All other anti-ERA women were members of the above mentioned groups. Among the "pro's," the one woman who was not a NOW member was well known to other NOW members in Maryland.

From the available pool of volunteers, only those who met one or more of the following criteria were selected for participation: 1) regular participation or election to office in one or more political organizations, 2) elected office holder (state or national level) with publicly stated ERA position, 3) appointed official (by Governor, Mayor, etc.) with publicly-stated ERA position, 4) coordinator of grass-roots feminist or anti-feminist organization, 5) voluntary or employed lobbyist working for feminist or anti-feminist legislation. Sample size was deliberately restricted because of the time-consuming nature of the interview technique.

Of the twelve participants finally selected, five of the anti-ERA women belonged to Eagle Forum and/or Stop ERA. The sixth opponent, as previously mentioned, was affiliated with the Conservative Caucus and Young ·Americans for Freedom, (organizations which have contributed time and money toward ERA's defeat). Two of these anti-ERA women were additionally coordinators of grass roots anti-feminist organizations (Pro-Morality Coalition, and Parents and Children Together).

Five of the ERA proponents were members of the National Organization for Women. One of these five was an elected official (state legislator); another was a lobbyist for Planned Parenthood. The remaining proponent was a gubernatorial appointment to the State Commission on Women.

As aforementioned, previous research has underlined the importance of religious ideology to position on ERA among female activists. Religious denomination and importance of religion to the respondent are used in these studies as measures of religious ideology, in order to recognize the multi-dimensionality of religion.[5]

It therefore seemed appropriate to supplement the interview schedule with an in-depth scale of religiosity. The Dimensions of Religious Ideology Scale,[6] which includes three sub-scales, orthodoxy, fanaticism, and importance, was chosen because it is both comprehensive and has been tested and validated.[7] The three sub-scales are comprised of six items each. Respondents rate each statement on Likert-type response scales, a score of 7 indicating strong agreement and of 1 indicating strong disagreement. Snell Putney and Russell Middleton designed these scales to assess the orthodoxy of religious beliefs, the fanaticism inspired by such beliefs and the importance of these beliefs to the individual's self-concept. The three scales together measure belief or ideological dimensions of religion and are generally considered the best single index of religiosity.[8]

Previous research also found religious involvement to be a significant indication of ERA preference, assessing whether each respondent was a church member.[9] To explore this variable further, we employ the Religious Orientation and Involvement Inventory.[10] In this inventory, associational involvement refers to participation in corporate worship.[11] This variable measures the relative frequency with which the individual has attended religious services in the last year. Communal involvement refers to the degree to which a person's primary group is restricted to members of her own religion.[12] This variable is measured by the proportion of the respondent's close friends who are of the same religion as the respondent.

Political ideology is also a very broad, multi-dimensional concept. In dealing with ERA position, it is logical to examine respondents' conceptions of "women's proper role" as one component of political ideology.

Although popular understanding often assumes the directionality of the relationship between ERA position and attitudes about women's role in society, this relationship has never been measured.

The Attitudes Toward Women Scale (AWS),[13] as Likert-type scale, contains statements about the rights and roles of women in such areas as vocational, educational and intellectual activities; dating behavior and etiquette; sexual behavior; and marital relationships. The shortened version of AWS has been found to correlate very highly with the longer form, which has been used extensively.[14]

Brady and Tedin[15] measured the political ideology of politically active ERA opponents by selected items from a scale of political conservatism. Our open-ended interviews encouraged respondents to explain their political ideology and ERA preference. The use of in-depth interviews to establish ideological correlates of political behavior has been used by several investigators.[16] The precedent for the use of in-depth interviews to explore political opinion with small groups was set by Brewster Smith, Jerome Bruner and Robert White.[17]

The semi-structured interviews addressed such issues as: 1) did respondents consider themselves politically active and how did they define politically active; 2) what had they done politically; 3) if their political views were the same as or different from their parents'; 4) the extent to which their respondents' political activity involved ERA; 5) other political issues with which they were concerned; 6) what they felt would happen, to themselves and to society, if the ERA were ratified? why?; 7) would their future political activity be determined by the outcome of the ERA campaign. This interview format was administered to individual respondents in one-hour sessions.

Results and Discussion

The anti-ERA women in our sample had an average age of 51, whereas the pro-ERA women had an average age of 43. This difference was not statistically significant. In contrast, an age difference was demonstrated by Tedin et al.,[23] with a larger sample. All anti-ERA women interviewed were married, excepting one widow; all but one were mothers. None of these women were self-supporting, except one who lived on inheritance income. Further, half of these women stated "homemaker" as their primary occupation. Of the "pros," three were married, one widowed and two single. Half were mothers.

All the pro-ERA women identified themselves with a profession. When interviewed, all but two of these women had full-time paid employment.

Of the two exceptions, one woman was pregnant and held a part-time position; the other was between jobs and obtained employment shortly afterward. This apparent life style difference is supported by Tedin et al., in their study: this difference in our sample however, did not seem to reflect the income level difference between the two groups that was previously found.[19]

Previous research has also shown a difference in the educational level of pro- and anti-ERA activists, with the "pro's" more educated on the whole than the "anti's."[20] Although our findings did not reveal education as a statistically significant differentiating variable, a clear pattern was evident. None of the anti-ERA women in this sample had college educations, save one who had a Master's degree. On the other hand, all but one of the pro-ERA respondents had graduate degrees; the exception currently attends law school.

Consequently, we have evidence that the pro- and anti-ERA women interviewed differed in life style, in that the "pro's" were largely professional women and the "anti's" were largely devoted to being wives and mothers. The investment of the "anti's" in tradition and of the "pro's" in change ostensibly makes sense; each group behaves politically in a way that appears to be life style affirming. The opinion of these authors is that this sensiblity is not the whole story, given the presence of married women with children in the pro-ERA group. Also, a simplistic life style explanation is refuted by the fact that human beings are confronted daily by events not life style affirming, without being motivated to political action.

Pro- and anti-groups were identical in denominational affiliation, each group consisting of one-third Jews, Catholics and Protestants. This does not support earlier findings that anti-ERA women are much more likely to belong to strongly conservative, fundamentalist denominations.[21]

Previous researchers have, however, acknowledged that their findings might have been reflective of the particular geographic location in which the studies were done. Fundamentalist denominations such as the Church of Christ are far more prevalent in Southern states than in the Northeast, where our interviews took place.

Although neither group differed in religious affiliation, each differed in religious involvement. "Anti's" reported attending religious services two or three times a month; "pro's" reported attending a few times a year or less ($p < .01$). "Anti's" reported that a greater proportion of their friends shared their religious convictions than did the "pro's" ($p < .01$). Anti-ERA women manifested significantly more religious orthodoxy ($p < .01$) and fanaticism ($p < .01$) than pro-ERA women; but neither group differed significantly in importance of religion. Both groups found religion to be important to them, although their interpretations of religion and of its impact on daily behavior differed. These findings suggested that the "anti's" interpreted their religion more literally than the "pro's" and believed more strongly that their religious views should be shared by others, as evidenced in the following quote:

> There are so many heresies flying around today with Catholic church and a lot of clergy are sort of giving their own opinions...I am watchful of the clergy to see that they follow the proper authority . . . acting according to the magesterium of the church.

Our findings support previous findings; the anti-ERA women surveyed here resembled the Religious Right in orientation.[22]

One of the determinants of support or opposition to ERA passage seems to be holding by an individual of traditional or nontraditional beliefs concerning women's "proper role." The Attitudes Toward Women Scale was administered to pro- and anti-ERA women with the expectation that their ERA preference reflected underlying differences in ideology about the role of women. As predicted, "anti's" held a conservative or traditional view of women's role, while "pro's" held a more liberal or feminsit view. The difference between group mean scores on the AWS was significant (p < .01), despite the small number of subjects. We may conclude that, at least among the women studied, differences in ERA preference reflect not only differences in life-style choice, but also strong ideological differences regarding women's role.

There was, however, evidence of sex-role inconsistency in the response of the anti-ERA women. All but one disagreed that "the intellectual leadership of a community should be largely in the hands of men." These women apparently endorse a politicized if traditional role for women. In fact, two of the "anti" women spoke of their efforts to politicize other women, reporting that they tell their friends: "If you're not willing to do anything, you have no right to bitch."

During the taped interviews, several "anti's" made comments indicating that cross sex-role behavior was desirable and that traditional female role behavior was not. One "anti" reported proudly that the women in her family were very strong and that her grandmother was "almost the man of the house." Another women confessed that if it had not been for her husband, she would have been a *typical housewife and dummy.* Another woman indicated that traditional female activity within her political organization was silly and boring, remarking that "worrying about when they were having their next banquet left me cold." Another claimed that non-political volunteer activity was "not her thing."

This apparent inconsistency indicated that these women are comfortable exercising power within the political sphere and encouraging others to do likewise. They seem less comfortable with exchanging gender-assigned tasks within the personal sphere. Therefore, they disagree strongly that the "intellectual leadership of a community should be largely in the hands of men" but completely endorse the notion that "it is ridiculous for a woman to run a locomotive and for a man to darn socks."[23]

Virginia Sapiro and Barbara Farah have argued against the myth that traditional women need shy away from political activity, indicating that the above-mentioned inconsistency is not inconsistent at all. "If an activity is relatively non-competitive, service oriented, and not in conflict with home and child we see no reason for the "traditional woman" to shy away from not only general participation, but leadership positions."[24] One anti-ERA woman, herself in a leadership role within the movement, explained that "we never allow our political activity to interfere with our husbands or children." This woman explained that when her political activity took her out of the home she prepared dinner well in advance and left detailed instructions for her oldest child to heat the dinner. "That way, no one will ever be inconvenienced."

The existence of conservative attitudes toward women's role among anti-ERA women is congruent with their religious orthodoxy, because most orthodox religious doctrines espouse traditional roles for women. Further, the relationship between orthodoxy, attitudes toward women, and opposition to the ERA is highlighted in the words of one Jewish anti-ERA woman:

> I decided to work against ratification of the ERA because if it were passed it would interfere with my son's right to keep an orthodox house.

This is not to imply that traditional religions have not endorsed strength and power in women as long as they were directed toward home and family. In other words, women may conform to traditional religious doctrine and still be powerful. The use of power, however, should be directed toward the area designated for women—the home and family.

The consistent polarizing of pro- and anti-ERA women regarding ERA position, attitudes toward women, religious ideology and involvement are probably related to more broad-based political ideologies. This claim is strongly supported by much of the literature on the radical right and the extreme left, as well as by our respondents' comments.

Radical rightists are reported to have a strong opposition to big government and to equalitarianism, and to have an exaggerated concern with a perceived breakdown in morality. "The American Right vocally opposes liberal sex mores, permissive child rearing, the use of drugs, departures from prevailing dress codes, and unconventional life styles. Members of the Right also tend to be atypically Republican in their party preferences."[25]

All six anti-ERA women in the sample were politically active within the conservative wing of the Republican party, several mentioning they had worked for the elections of Goldwater and Reagan. One "anti" respondent reported the following episode concerning her early political activity:

> When Goldwater was defeated...everything was wrong. I felt almost as badly as I had when I thought there wasn't a God! Because I thought, if you put that man in there he'll get us straightened out.
>
> I had all these young people organized working for Goldwater, and when he was defeated I thought "what am I going to tell them?" They'll be so disappointed, and it's terrible to disappoint young people.

Another anti-ERA woman was originally inspired to political activism when she read Goldwater's *The Conscience of a Conservative*. She enthusiastically recalled that this was the first time she had seen her very thoughts so well articulated by a political figure.

Opposition to big government or anti-statism was demonstrated by many of our anti-ERA women, and is in fact a leading theme of Phyllis Schlafly's *The Power of the Positive Woman*.[26] One anti-ERA woman in our sample expressed her anti-statism thusly: "I'm totally concerned about government intervening in our lives. I just feel that we're being surrounded by rules and regulations; you almost feel that you are being strangled." Another "anti" offered the following analysis: Our country is slipping to the left so far and we're giving up our free enterprise. The government's messing into everybody's business. I've just got to get the government off our backs."

One of our ERA opponents was a founding member of a grass roots organization called "The Pro-Morality Coalition," which has as one of its aims the end of sex education in schools. The issue of sex education was also salient to another opponent, who dated her political activity from her daughter's exposure to a junior high school film which included masturbation and lesbian life style as topics. Summarizing her complaints about sex education in the schools she offered the following: "I am very much opposed to sex education. Since sex education was piloted we've seen all these teen-age pregnancies. There is a concerted effort to make children confused and lost." This "concerted effort," in the opinion of the respondent, was directed through such school programs as values clarification, sex education and education on drug and alcohol abuse. Yet a third opponent was particularly angered by the introduction of what she termed "moral relativism" into the school curricula.

The right wing's opposition to departures from prevailing dress codes is vividly illustrated by the proud assertion of one of our "anti" women that she insists her son wear a crew cut and that both her children "dress nicely." She further reported that she admonished them to steer clear of "hoods and bums" and "drug takers." She explained that "we knew that it was not right to let our boys wear long hair. We didn't like a boy to look like a girl."

Anti-Communism, at home and abroad, and foreign policy were also leading concerns of the ERA opponents. One "anti" was strong in her support for what she termed our free enterprise system and asserted that "I know we're going socialistic." Two "anti's" believed that much information is being withheld from the American people, one claiming that "the military has been muzzled." One ERA opponent cited the communist infiltration in Cuba as a good foreign policy lesson for the United States, suggesting that "the people in Cuba are now enslaved, who had been free before Castro."

All anti-ERA women endorsed the need to put America first, if not exclusively. One "anti" remarked: "We should concentrate on our own country and not this world outlook... I feel the defense of our nation should be put first." All "anti's" also reported they were very much opposed to "giving away" the Panama Canal.

The pro-ERA women, on the other hand, do not view the political climate as do the anti-ERA women. Rather than fearing the power of federal government to intrude upon their lives, they want to broaden the power of the federal government to fight sex discrimination. This view was well expressed by a "pro" women who said:

> Federal legislation can address women's issues quicker... As the majority of women will be alone for at least part of their lives, and must live as independent entities, they need laws to assist them and the guarantee of government looking out for the rights of women.

Another "pro" woman, herself intending to run for political office in the future, talked at great length about her role in fighting sex discrimination by using government mechanisms. The fact of the matter is that the ERA proponents do not see how sex discrimination can ever be halted without the benefit of a national commitment, a national amendment and nationally-empowered bodies to enforce the law.

There was one area, however, in which the "pro's" did not welcome government intervention, that being the right to abortion. While many of the anti-ERA women are opposed to abortion, their sentiment was not shared by the "pro's" in this sample. One proponent is a lobbyist for Planned Parenthood; and many proponents mentioned that they disliked the anti-abortion stand taken by many ERA opponents. The "anti's" in our sample saw abortion as murder, while the "pros" saw it as a woman's right to choose. The "anti's" self-admitted concern is for the fetus or, as many suggested, the "unborn child," whereas the "pro's" concern is for the woman. The sentiments of the "pro" women in our sample were reflected in the self-reported reactions of one woman to the statements against abortion by a male state legislator. This respondent challenged the legislator's "right to decide about an issue that could potentially threaten a women's life." Except for the topic of abortion, other morality issues were not specifically brought up by the ERA proponents, suggesting a "moral breakdown" is not a salient issue for these women.

If sex education and foreign policy were major concerns of the "anti's," the ERA proponents expressed far more concern with civil rights and social welfare issues. One "pro" discussed her long standing involvement with the National Association for the Advancement of Colored People. All "pro's" expressed concern that everyone have equal treatment and equal opportunity, regardless of sex, race and socio-economic level. The contrast between "pro's" and "anti's" on social welfare issues can be seen in the following self-reports. One "anti" reported that she had tried to be a social worker but "couldn't handle people getting welfare checks who didn't deserve them." One "pro" woman, herself a state legislator, worked on getting higher welfare grants under Aid to Families with Dependent Children. This was one of her major concerns in the state legislature.

The "anti's" were typically Republican; the ERA proponents sampled were all Democrats. Three proponents were highly active in the Democratic party. One proponent had been actively involved in the Democratic party on the state level for ten years. She recounts her political history as follows: "I was selected as a delegate to the Democratic convention in 1972 and served on the state Federal Committee, which is the governing body of the state party." Her major concern was "women having equal voice in political parties." Regarding her own role as a convention delegate in 1972 she says, "I was elected, but in most parts of the state women didn't have equal access to the selection process."

Sapiro and Farah note that many women enter politics through the long accepted tradition of volunteerism. As they suggested, "a woman who has served her time licking stamps and making phone calls may simply develop the desire to contribute to her organization in a slightly more challenging and interesting fashion."[27] Two of our "pro's" identified their own commitment to the Democratic party as something which developed from their earlier days as volunteers.

One ERA proponent recounted her own political evolution:

> I started out primarily in support functions for the political activity of my husband in the Democratic party, and took it from there....It depends on how you define political. Volunteer work is an excellent example. No one would fault a woman who needed the help of her legislator for the good of her community...How far the woman goes in political activity depends on the support of her family.

This woman reported that she parted company from the supportive role when she attended a Democratic state convention and discovered "I could speak English" in a way that was articulate and persuasive, and "this was acknowledged by my husband."

Another proponent originally worked as a volunteer for other Democratic candidates. She did so for fifteen years, beginning in high school. She reports that she increased her level of political participation "from handing out leaflets to running for office when I was involved in the political campaign of a very close friend."

ERA proponents were not concerned with "unconventional life-styles," preferring instead to focus on expanded life styles and goals for women. They did not indicate concern about their children's dress or hair length, nor did they mention concern about "deviant" life styles.

The predicted outcomes of ERA ratification/defeat mentioned by our respondents are clearly congruent with their overall political ideology. "Anti" women unanimously predict a chaotic society rampant with governmental intervention and a widespread breakdown of traditional morality if the ERA is ratified. "Pro" women see governmental intervention as essential to safeguard gains already made by women and to provide the legal basis for further advancement. The "anti's" position is clearly consistent with their general political conservatism and strongly orthodox religious beliefs. The freedom envisioned by the "pro's" is consistent with their general political liberalism.

Much of the ERA opposition stems from the belief that the amendment is "anti-family." One "anti," in describing personal losses if ERA is ratified, says simply: "There would be a breakdown of the traditional family structure, and I would lose my freedom to *choose* to raise a family or to see my children *choose* to enter service." Another "anti" offered the belief that she would "lose the right to be identified and treated as a woman." As she put it "I don't want to stoop to equality." A third woman paradoxically offered the following: "Woman, their families, society will *all* lose much under ERA. States will lose their jurisdiction over the most personal areas of our lives: marriage, divorce, family and child support, family and property rights and inheritance taxes."

Yet another woman mentioned the loss of "my daughters, since they would all qualify for the draft and combat duty." The military issue was also salient to an opponent who quoted her husband's dying words: "As long as there is breath in your body you fight the ERA because if women are ever drafted and sent into combat civilization as we know it is gone." One woman simply said that ERA ratification would result in "a chaotic society and a giant step toward socialism."

ERA opponents predicted a brighter future if ERA were not ratified. One said "I would have peace of mind in knowing that any unjust law which unfairly discriminates against women could be changed and that fair and just discrimination which protects women would be retained." Another emphatically suggested "My confidence in people would be reinstated. It would mean a defeat for the liberal press, the liberal newspapers and the liberal politicians: Dregs, all!" A third said, "If ERA's defeated women will *retain* the legal benefits and protections conferred upon us as the bearers of children." A fourth respondent confessed "I am not willing to give up the privilege, or right, to be a woman for the right to be treated like a man. Women would suffer many losses in the jobs, breakdown of the home and on and on...."

"Anti's" unanimously see no losses if the ERA is defeated. As one "anti" summed it up: "Not one damn thing." The central themes apparent in the above comments are clearly the threat of ERA ratification to women's perceived privileges, to family and the country as a whole. The specifics of how the ERA would actually threaten the status quo are not offered anywhere by the respondents in their interviews.

The consequences of ERA ratification, as perceived by proponents, were summarized in the words of one respondent: "There will be a higher standard by which laws and policies which discriminate against women will be held to." Similarly, another "pro" stated: "There will be mandated equal access. I will have the knowledge that there is one federal law rather than all the separate points of law and legislation that are open to interpretation." A third woman admitted that:

> I would gain the satisfaction that I was part of the ratification effort. Changes that would occur for all women would affect me also. I would retain the freedom to chose a life style without being forced to do what society expects.

Expanding further, one woman explained as follows: "The figures show that women are not gaining economically. If we need to go case by case the going is going to be rough. The direction the Supreme Court is taking— we're going to take a long time and we may be lost." Regarding individual legislation, this same respondent continued: "We're still depending on the men to get our things through...Even though we have a state ERA, our legislators are dragging their heels because we're now hitting home in an area that men really resent, which is property."

Discussing the specifics of ERA impact, this woman also suggested the following:

> If I were married, there would be the issue of Social Security or if I were divorced—but I don't have that problem. As a widow, I am treated very differently than as a married woman. As a widow, you are automatically a person. These problems will continue if ERA is not ratified.

A "pro" who is a state legislator commented that, under the current non-ratified status of ERA, "when the Supreme Court evaluates laws which are discriminatory the people who justify sex discrimination don't have to justify it very much in order for it to be okay." One "pro," a gubernatorial appointee to her State Commission on the Status of Women at that time of the interview, suggested that "ERA ratification is critical because court cases and legislation can be removed or acted upon negatively as they are opened to interpretation." The ERA proponents fear that the court is not a dependable route to take in order to permanently assure women's rights.[28]

Another common theme sounded by the proponents was that they termed the "psychological impact" of passage. As Jo Freeman has suggested, "its most valuable effect at this point will be the psychological victory it will provide of declaring women constitutionally equal to men.''[29] Losing the ratification fight would therefore probably be a psychological setback. One proponent said that if the ERA fails, ''we will not be affirmed in our rights to have rights.'' All ERA respondents pointed out that because the ERA has become so prominent and controversial, non-ratification ''will be perceived as a setback for the women's movement.'' The political consequence of ''failure to ratify can convince legislators that the movement has no clout.'' Interestingly, two pro-ERA women felt that the amendment would not be ratified, despite the time extension granted by Congress. All the proponents insisted that they would remain politically active, regardless of the amendment's final outcome.

Although the question was not directly asked, four of the pro-ERA women offered their perceptions of the beliefs of the anti-ERA women. These observations correspond in some degree to the ''anti's'' objections to ERA ratification. For instance, one proponent remarked: ''ERA has become a battleground and a symbol for what are perceived as feminist causes. A lot of people are turned off by 'women's libbers' and would vote against ERA because they don't like 'women's libbers.'''

Another proponent speculated on fear and misunderstanding of the consequences of ERA ratification among its opponents:

> People misunderstand what ERA will actually do. Phyllis Schlafly, bright as she is, does not really understand what it will not do. Most of the people against it are scared of something, and for each person that's something different. The fear might be that women will have to go into men's rooms to go to the bathroom or the fear might be that women will be called into war.

Finally, one proponent suggested the following: ''Women working against ERA are buying the myth; they really believe that if they stay home, are good homemakers, and behave themselves, that God and country will take care of them. . . That's not the case.''

In comparing the two groups, the ''pro's'' appear to have some sympathy for or understanding toward the kinds of people who might reject ERA. The ''anti's'' did not appear to have the same kind of empathy for ERA proponents.

Regarding the discussion of the consequences of ERA ratification or defeat, the proponents were much more detailed in their analysis than the ''anti's.'' The ''anti's'' spoke globally about a catastrophic move to socialism, chaos, loss of privacy, loss of financial security and even the loss of civilization as we know it. They were nebulous, however, in explaining how these catastrophies could result from ERA ratification.

The "pro's," on the other hand, made relatively modest claims for the success of ERA ratification. Although ratification was clearly important to them, none expected a miraculous change for women. In the words of one proponent: "Even with ERA ratification, changing attitudes won't be easy. However, we will have the clout of the law behind us." In their discussion of the consequences of ERA ratification, the "pro's" were far more specific than the "anti's." They spoke to the need for legislation in areas such as social security, divorce, employment, property rights, etc. They further tried to explain how ERA would ensure such rights through its blanket protection of women.

Conclusion

The key difference between the pro- and anti-ERA women sampled here is clearly an ideological one. The "anti's" manifest many of the concerns of the New Right, including grave concern over a moral breakdown of society, suspicion of Communist infiltration, concern about governmental interference (in selected policy areas), paramilitarism and an overriding concern for the preservation for the traditional family. Within this context, and perhaps only within this context, this group's ERA position is consistent and predictable.

The pro-ERA position is also consistent and predictable within the ideological context. The "pro's" focused upon egalitarianism, expanded lifestyle options, rights and responsibilities. Their policy concerns ranged from giving women a greater voice within the political sphere to freedom to choose on abortion, to NAACP involvement and to legislation to raise grants to families with dependent children. They are clearly people to be described as "liberal."

Within the context of each group's ideology, the perceived consequences of ERA ratification or defeat also makes sense. The "anti's," for their part, see chaos and socialism, loss of compensatory privileges, and the death of the traditional family. For them ERA passage is not perceived as a benefit. An interesting difference between the "pro's" and the "anti's" is that the "pro's," although certainly hoping for ERA ratification, have a less extreme version of a society without the ERA. Where the "anti's" see ERA ratification as socialistic, the "pro's" did not see ERA defeat as indicative of fascism. ERA proponents most frequently mention that ERA defeat would be a psychological setback and would lengthen the process for achieving their rights. They nonetheless felt that ERA defeat would not threaten their life styles or pursuit of their goals.

The "anti's" feel that with ERA's defeat their position in life will be more secure. They see their family structure as being less threatened and governmental intervention directed more toward what are perceived as more appropriate goals. ERA proponents feel they have much to gain by establishing a high standard to secure women's rights and thereby protect recent gains made by the women's movement. In particular the "pro's" stress the undependability and the slowness of securing rights through the courts on a case-by-case basis and through piecemeal legislation. A blanket federal amendment is thus perceived as desirable.

The Attitudes Toward Women Scale differentiated between the "pro's" and the "anti's" with "pro's" being more liberal and "anti's" more conservative. The "anti's," however, strongly endorse their own participation in political matters, supporting the contention of Sapiro and Farah that politics need not be closed off to the traditional woman. By using the in-depth interview technique, we were able to explore this contention further. "Anti" women often endorsed cross sex-role behavior and sometimes even put down traditional female behavior.

The use of a milti-dimensional scale to measure religiousity both confirmed and questioned previous research. The confirmation lay in our finding that religiosity was related to ERA preference. In addition, however, we found that anti-ERA women were both more fanatical and orthodox than the "pro's," attended church services more frequently than "pro's," and reported that most of their friends shared their religious convictions. The "pro's," on the other hand, did not report that most of their friends shared their religious conviction. An interesting similarity still emerged. Both opponents and proponents said that religion was important to them. Although previous research suggested a relationship between religious denomination and ERA preference, our study uncovered no such relationship.

Pro- and anti-ERA women in our study are greatly polarized along firmly-established ideological dimensions. Both groups vow to stay in the political arena, in the words of both "anti" and "pro," "to the last breath." Because both groups appear to spring from firmly-entrenched ideological traditions, both will undoubtedly find future and current issues around which we can expect further polarization.

FOOTNOTES

1. David W. Brady and Kent L. Tedin, "Ladies in Pink: Religion and Political Ideology in the Anti-ERA Movement," *Social Science Quarterly*, 56 (March 1976), 564–75.

2. Kent L. Tedin, "Religious Preference and Pro/Anti Activism on the Equal Rights Amendment Issue," *Pacific Sociological Review*, 21 (January 1978), 55-66.

3. Kent L. Tedin et al., "Social Background and Political Differences Between Pro and Anti ERA Activists," *American Politics Quarterly*, 5 (July 1977), 395-408.

4. Fred N. Kerlinger, *Foundations of Behavioral Research* (New York: Holt, Rinehart and Winston, 1973).

5. Brady and Tedin, "Ladies in Pink"; Tedin et al., "Social Background and Political Differences;" Tedin, "Religious Preference and Pro/Anti Activism."

6. Snell Putney and Russell Middleton, "Dimensions and Correlates of Religious Ideologies," *Social Forces*, 39 (May 1960), 235-90.

7. John P. Robinson and Philip R. Shaver, *Measures of Social Psychological Attitudes* (Ann Arbor, Michigan: Institute for Social Resources, 1973).

8. *Ibid.*

9. Brady and Tedin, "Ladies in Pink"; Tedin et al., "Social Background and Political Differences."

10. Gerhard Emmanuel Lenski, *The Religious Factor* (New York: Doubleday, 1963).

11. Robinson and Shaver, *Measures of Social Psychological Attitudes.*

12. *Ibid.*, p. 667.

13. Janet T. Spence and Robert Helmreich, "The Attitudes Toward Women Scale: An Objective Instrument to Measure Attitudes Toward the Rights and Roles of Women in Contemporary Society," *Catalog of Selected Documents in Psychology*, 2 (1972), 66-77; Janet T. Spence, Robert Helmreich and Joy Staff, "A Short Version of the Attitudes Toward Women Scale," *Bulletin Psychon Society*, 2 (1973), 219-20.

14. Janet T. Spence and Robert Helmreich, *Masculinity and Femininity* (Austin: University of Texas Press, 1978).

15. Brady and Tedin, "Ladies in Pink."

16. Theodore W. Odorno et al., *The Authoritarian Personality* (New York: Harper, 1950); Robert Lane, *Political Ideology* (New York: Free Press, 1952); Kathleen McCourt, *Working Class Women* (Bloomington: University of Indiana Press, 1977).

17. M. Brewster Smith, Jerome S. Bruner and Robert W. White, *Opinions and Personality* (New York: Wiley, 1956).

18. Tedin, Brady et al., "Social Background and Political Differences."

19. See *Ibid.*

20. *Ibid.*

21. See Tedin, "Religious Preference and Pro/Anti Activism."

22. Brady and Tedin, "Ladies in Pink."

23. See Spence and Helmreich, "The Attitudes Toward Women Scale"; Spence, Helmreich and Staff, "A Short Version."

24. Virginia Sapiro and Barbara Farah, "New Pride and Old Prejudice," *Women & Politics*, 1 (Spring 1980), 17-18.

25. Brady and Tedin, "Ladies in Pink," p. 565.

26. Phyllis Schlafly, *The Power of the Positive Woman* (New York: Harcourt, Brace, 1977).

27. Sapiro and Farah, "New Pride and Old Prejudice," p. 34.

28. See also Janet K. Boles, *The Politics of the Equal Rights Amendment* (New York: Longman, 1979), p. 37.

29. Jo Freeman, *The Politics of Women's Liberation* (New York: McKay, 1975), p. 238.

COALITION POLITICS:
A CASE STUDY OF AN ORGANIZATION'S
APPROACH TO A SINGLE ISSUE

Nancy Douglas Joyner

ABSTRACT. This article provides a case study of the contemporary nature of organizational coalitions for political purposes. It focuses on one organization's—the American Association of University Women—efforts to secure ratification of the equal rights amendment by the state legislature in Illinois through concerted efforts in a central project composed of other diversified groups and organizations. The analysis includes a general overview of the nature and problems of coalitions, an historical perspective of the AAUW and the ERA and the use of organizational resources to achieve a common goal. It concludes by offering some suggestions for future organizational cooperative efforts.

Introduction

The contemporary nature of organizational coalitions is both promising and perplexing. Building coalitions at best provides an opportunity to increase political clout to its apex, thereby producing a synergistic effect, especially for smaller, less politically involved organizations. Yet, at worst, the coalition process is oftentimes looked upon as a waste of time, requiring too many meetings and resource allocations which more frequently than not produce "all talk and no real action."

Respecting the drive to ratify the equal rights amendment in Illinois, the perceived necessity for organizational coalescence to achieve ratification became evident by late 1970. Realization that the only remaining Northern state to ratify the ERA still might not do so unless extraordinary political pressure was brought to bear on its elected legislative officials became the catalyst for launching an aggressive effort toward ratification through coalition politics. This paper presents a case study of the experiences of one organization—the American Association of University Women (AAUW)—and its efforts to ratify the ERA, as well as discusses the nature and characteristics of coalitions themselves, analyzes the specific problems at-

Nancy Douglas Joyner is national First Vice President of The American Association of University Women, and Member of Corporate Board of Directors ERAmerica, 172C Georgetown Road, Charlottesville, VA 22901.

57

tached to ERA ratification efforts in the state of Illinois, and makes some concluding remarks *vis-a-vis* the future of nongovernmental organizational coalitions for single issue purposes.

Nature of the Problem of Coalitions

In his work, *Building Coalitions*, Andrew M. Greeley enumerates three types of coalitions: long range, short range and *ad hoc*.[1] Each type is distinguished by certain characteristics, goals and means of maintenance. Long range coalitions, i.e., the convention of groups for a protracted period of time, do not currently apply to the issue of the equal rights amendment. These coalitions are best exemplified by more readily available examples, such as established political parties whose efforts to coalesce segments of the population with similar goals are carried out over a long period of time.[2]

Short range coalitions, on the other hand, "may be the beginnings of an alliance for which the participants think there may be long-range possibilities,"[3] but this is not a major criterion for their existence. Greeley asserts that short range coalitions are brought together for "limited purposes" and "do not assume a broad range of common values."[4] Significantly, short range coalitions frequently build upon the "temporary broadening of already existing long range coalitions."[5] Thus, while organizations in the women's movement have not always aligned themselves with various labor, religious, civil rights or other orgaizations, many diverse groups have found themselves to be compatible members of alliances for the ERA. The Labor Rally for the ERA held in Chicago in April, 1980, aptly attests to the coalition of some labor and women's organizations commited to the ERA.

Another example of short range coalition efforts can be seen in the combination of what Greeley refers to as *ad hoc* coalitions, which are joined together for a specific, less permanent purpose.[6] *Ad hoc* coalitions are abundant in the ERA ratification movement. These would include a number of religious organizations, such as Catholics Act for ERA, Mormons for ERA, Priests for Equality and the Illinois Religious Committee for the ERA, as well as groups such as the National Business Council for ERA.

Ad hoc coalitions can be found on the national, state and local levels, and many have been formed as coordinating mechanisms for only one purpose—ratification of the Equal Rights Amendment—with the undergirding assumption that the coalition will dissolve once the mutual goal has been achieved.

It is not surprising, then, that short range as well as *ad hoc* coalitions in support of the ERA, can be found in virtually all of the fifteen unratified states, and in many states which face possible attempts by legislatures to rescind their respective passages of the ERA. Difficulties with achieving ratification have spanned all levels of government and have necessitated responses on various organizational levels in return.[7]

Earl Latham has stated that the primary social values of modern society are fulfilled through groups.[8] The groups "may be simple in structure...or intricate meshes of associated, federated, combined, consolidated, merged, or amalgamated units and subunits of organization, fitted together to perform the divided and assigned parts of a common purpose to which the components are dedicated."[9]

Even within a single organization, it is often difficult to coordinate multiple activities through different subunits designed virtually for a common purpose. In the case of the AAUW, three structural levels must be spanned: the Association (or national), the state division and the branch. The types of activities each level performs on behalf of ERA ratification in Illinois differ in scope, degree and intensity. Hence, the emergence of new coalition—the Illinois ERA Ratification Project—necessitated a significant shift in resource usage and also coordination carfully tailored to the limits of authority granted to each participating organization. A more thorough historical as well as contemporary analysis of AAUW's experiences regarding the ERA sheds light on the phenomenon of coalition building.

An Historical Perspective of AAUW and the ERA

The American Association of University Women was founded in 1881 as an organization of university women graduates dedicated to three overarching purposes: 1) the advancement of women in society, especially in the area of education; 2) the personal growth and development of the individual; and 3) the utilization of the talents of university women to contribute in a meaningful way to the community.[10] In sum, AAUW's establishment was promoted by a willingness of educated women to do practical work during an era in which women were not only discouraged from attaining a college education, but also were frowned upon for even attempting to become gainfully employed outside the home. The organization prides itself on its ability to study issues circumspectly before embarking upon a course of action to achieve a desired goal.

As early as 1923 when the equal rights amendment was first introduced to the U.S. Congress, the Association's Committee on Legislation began to study the issue but took no action on it.[11] During that year AAUW members concentrated their attention on other policy questions considered

to be of more immediate and special interest than the ERA to the membership, such as civil service reform, the International Court of Justice, a
separate Cabinet-level Department of Education and the proposed child
welfare amendment.

The AAUW did not begin its support of the ERA until 1971, when,
at its biennial national convention in Dallas, AAUW delegates voted to place
the equal rights amendment on its legislative program agenda.[12] After nearly
five decades, it became apparent to the delegates that the ponderous, rather
arduous process of altering existing state and federal legislation which
discriminated unfairly on the basis of sex had been less than successful.
While great expansion had come in the roles, choices and opportunities
available to the modern woman of the 1970s, there nonetheless had been
little real progress made the issue of inferior legal treatment of women.[13]

By 1975, AAUW realized that its support for the ERA necessitated a
more active and vigorous advocacy role.[14] Delegates at the Seattle national
biennial convention that year voted that ratification of the ERA should be
hearlded as the Association's top priority.[15] At the next two subsequent national conventions in 1975 and 1977, AAUW delegated reaffirmed and rein-
forced their support of the ERA.[16] Under the mandate provided by those
conventions, the AAUW Legislative Program and Resolutions for 1979-81
included the following;

> AAUW supports measures that preserve and protect the basic legal
> and human rights of all individuals. To guarantee these rights we sup-
> port: Ratification of the Equal Rights Amendment...[and]...AAUW
> reaffirms as its highest priority ratification of the Equal Rights Amend-
> ment and will continue to commit appropriate personnel and funds
> to that goal...AAUW...deplores the failure of legislatures of the
> unratified states—Alabama, Arizona, Arkansas, Florida, Georgia, Il-
> linois, Louisiana, Mississippi, Missouri, Nevada, North Carolina,
> Oklahoma, South Carolina, Utah, and Virginia—to ratify the Equal
> Rights Amendment and reaffirms its stand taken in 1977 against
> holding national or regional conventions in unratified states...[17]

In addition to carrying out the convention mandate on the Association
level, state divisions and branches both are bound by the policies established
by their convention delegates.[18] It is to one state division's experiences in
action programs designed to ratify the ERA that this paper now turns.

The Illinois AAUW-ERA Experience

As of April, 1980, the Illinois State Division of the AAUW consisted of some 9,000 members located in all sectors of the state, It is internally divided into five districts for the purpose of representation, communication and organizational services, with a total of ninety-one local branches. All members are volunteers and are graduates of colleges and universities. They elect their own officers on the local level and subsequently send delegates to annual division and biennial association conventions for the purpose of electing officers and determining relevant policies. The Illinois AAUW's *Directory and Bylaws* for 1979-80 states the division's motto, "Interacting to Impact,"[19] and suggests a circular design representing movement of the volunteer member to the branch, the division and association levels as they impact on society as a whole. The first page of the *Directory* clearly states that "The highest priority of the American Association of University Women is the ratification of the Equal Rights Amendment."[20] This policy of the AAUW was reaffirmed at Illinois AAUW's 1980 annual meeting. Since 1972, ratification of the ERA has been the major human rights issue espoused in the agenda of the Illinois AAUW's legislative program.[21]

To carry out the ERA policy of the Illinois AAUW, an Ad Hoc Equal Rights Amendment Task Force was established and has operated since 1972. Its members have been active in letter writing to representatives of the Illinois General Assembly, lobbying in various legislators' home districts as well as in the Illinois capital of Springfield, participating in an ERA vigil each day while the legislature is in session and other similar advocacy activities. The Ad Hoc Task Force serves as a coordinating mechanism for the Division and solicits the assistance of the branch members to complement these actions.[22]

Additionally, because the AAUW is a broad-based, diversified organization of female college and university graduates, the Illinois AAUW's program reflects long-standing organizational interests in education, cultural relations, international affairs, the community and the legal advancement of women in society.[23] To enact specific policy goals in these areas, AAUW frequently participates in coalition efforts. Illinois AAUW, for example, belongs to several coalitions approved by its membership, maintains organizational affiliation and sends representatives to such groups as the Illinois Arts Council, the Illinois Environmental Council, the Illinois Commission on the Status of Women, the Illinois State Board of Education and ERA Illinois.[24]

In the latter area, an appointed representative of Illinois AAUW regularly participates in the activities of ERA Illinois, an ad hoc coalition of several educational, labor, religious, social civil rights and other nongovernmental organizations. ERA Illinois has thus provided an important umbrella coalition for organizational support of the amendment, primarily because of its clearinghouse ability to coordinate information and to serve as an interorganizational communications network.

By 1979, however, it had become apparent that an additional vehicle was needed to enhance the individual efforts of organizations. A new coalition, known as the Illinois ERA Ratification Project, was established to coordinate day-to-day advocacy activities in Illinois and to serve as the focal point of the campaign's organization. The nature and significance of this important coalition effort deserves further elaboration.

Groups Joining Groups: The Illinois ERA Ratification Project

The impetus for the Illinois ERA Ratification Project largely grew out of the success achieved by the National Organization for Women (NOW) in its well organized and coordinated campaign efforts to achieve an extension of the time period for states to consider ratification.[25] Through the leadership of NOW, many organizations such as the AAUW agreed temporarily to put aside the individual differences on organizational structures, policies and agendas to concentrate on one single, clearly defined overriding goal, namely to apply effective, collective pressure on Congress to approve extension of the ERA ratification deadline.[26]

How were various organizations brought together in the ERA Ratification Project within a single instead of on the federal Congressional level? Why was it necessary to enlarge the already existing, extensive activities of pro-ERA groups in Illinois?

Despite previous efforts of several hundred organizations in support of the ERA, the Illinois General Assembly has failed to ratify ERA by its own standard since first considering ERA in 1972. The Illinois standard for ratification of any Constitutional amendment is governed under two provisions: Article 14, Section 4 of the Illinois Constitution, and Legislative Rule 42. Section 4 of the state's Constitution reads in relevant part:

> ...the affirmative vote of three-fifths of the members elected to each house of the General Assembly shall be required to request Congress to call a Federal Constitutional Convention, to ratify a proposed amendment to the Constitution of the United States, or to call a State Convention to ratify a proposed amendment to the Constitution of the United States.[27]

Rule 42 further specifies that: (d) No such resolution (proposing changes to the Constitution of the U.S. or of Illinois, respectively) shall pass except upon an affirmative vote of 107 members; (e) The provisions of this rule may be suspended only upon affirmative vote of 107 members.[28]

No doubt exists that the provision for an "extraordinary majority"—two-thirds of *all* elected legislators—has prevented ERA's ratification in Illinois. The exact votes and relevant dates are documented in the appendix to this paper.[29] ERA has passed in one or more houses of the General Assembly on several occasions since 1972 by a majority vote, but never simultaneously and not in both houses under the supermajority vote standard.

The work of the ERA Ratification Project, then, was to overcome this extraordinary encumbrance through a massive, in-depth campaign to persuade Illinois legislators to vote for the amendment. The campaign was to be conducted in a manner similar to that of a major presidential campaign including: detailed analysis of the entire state's political atmosphere; exact information on legislators' past ERA voting records and or commitment of new officials to the ERA; targeting of specific districts; engaging constituents in massive lobbying activities, such as letter writing and educational outreach programs; and impacting upon primary and general elections in favor of pro-ERA candidates.[30]

The last area—working for the election of supportive ERA candidates—was an area in which AAUW could not participate. Under its current operating rules, AAUW neither endorses nor supports political candidates in partisan elections. It freely makes available to its membership information on candidate voting records on issues of concern, but this is done strictly on a non-partisan basis. AAUW's inability to participate in electoral activities was not a hindrance to affiliation in the ERA Ratification Project. Considering the tremendous amount of organization and planning to be done, there was ample opportunity to engage actively in other phases of the political process.

Over the years, successful coalition efforts by organizations advocating ERA have been hampered by several factors not unfamiliar to scholars of interest groups and coalitions. Since AAUW had not initiated the ERA Ratification Project (a modest office had been rented and a small staff hired by the National Organization for Women), it was necessary to determine how AAUW might reasonably contribute to the total ratification project's objectives while still retaining its own identity as an association. During the late fall and winter of 1979, AAUW conducted a pilot project in Chicago to assess how it might best serve the interests of its own membership, as well as augment the Association's goal of ratification by participation in the

ERA Ratification Project. Several weeks were spent working with officers of the Illinois AAUW, members of the Ad Hoc AAUW ERA Task Force, members of branches and other supporters of ERA, as individuals and through other organizations, including labor, religious, other women's, civil rights, political, civic and business groups.[31]

The result of these efforts was a decision on how AAUW could join the ERA Ratification Project and still contribute to its own political and educational process. Norman Ornstein and Shirley Elder have posited that "groups vary widely in their motivations, interests, memberships, leaderships, budgets, and scopes of activity."[32] Thus, when individual groups unite in coalition efforts, each participating member must determine what quantity and quality of resources will be contributed to the coalition's unified effort to achieve a common goal. Ornstein and Elder put it very succinctly:

> The combination of a group's goals, focus of activity motivation, mix of resources, and skill at using them—along with the nature of the government institutions and the motivations and viewpoints of the government decisionmakers—determine the political influence of the group.[33]

Political influence results from an admixture of the power components which an organization brings to bear through a coalition effort. These include physical, organizational, political, motivational and intangible resources.

In terms of physical resources, primarily size and financial backing, AAUW's participation in the ERA Ratification Project would be predicted on voluntary contributions on the Association level through the AAUW-ERA Fund. In addition, the AAUW Board of Directors voted at its November, 1979, meeting to adopt a coordinated program focus of "Action for Equity."[34] The new rubric embraced a two-pronged approach to the problems women face today in securing legal, economic, social, educational and political equity. In this endeavor, the Program Development Committee worked diligently to develop member materials and action-oriented ideas to study and address more fully the questions of achieving equity in general, with the ERA Ratification Task Force serving as the advocacy/action arm of the Association to strive toward passage in the unratified states. A large portion of existing program funds and staff time were devoted to the former goal of equity education, while the entire thrust of the voluntary funds, generated through the ERA Ratification Task Force's fund raising drives, were directed to activities in the unratified states, primarily Illinois. Augmenting the program and funding directives of AAUW is its exceptionally large size relative to other voluntary women's organizations: 190,000 members nationally, with nearly 9,000 of these in Illinois, providing AAUW with impressive physical resource to embellish the coalition efforts.[35]

In addition to the physical resources of money and membership size, AAUW also contributes to the ERA Ratification Project in terms of organizational resources, which include its nearly one-hundred year history of studying issues prior to taking action as an organization. Because AAUW is so large in size and diversified in membership characteristics, its members encompass a broad spectrum of political views, socio-economic background and interests, While this diversity has been a source of internal strength for a multi-based, program-oriented organization, it does not always lend itself to rapid mobilization of resources for political action. Thus, although members fully participate in the decision-making process which determines Association policies, a member is more likely to join AAUW for the personal and educational enrichment the company of other educated women affords. The desire to take more interest in the political process as a means of achieving advancement for women in society is more likely to materialize after membership has been attained.[36]

AAUW's substantive expertise, as Ornstein and Elder have phrased it, relates to its ability "to command facts, figures, and technical information in support of its positions..."[37] As an organization, AAUW's leadership over the years has gradually evolved from individuals committed more to some phases of program—such as the Educational Foundation Programs which provided over a million dollars in funding for women scholars in 1979-80—to commitment to all facets of diverse programming, including lobbying on legislative priority items such as the ERA. As an organization of volunteer women, AAUW faces similar problems to that of other volunteer organizations, namely the limited time available for community service by most women today.[38] One serious problem which has hitherto impeded the pro-ERA movement in Illinois as well as in other unratified states has been the inability of volunteers to devote the full time and attention needed to fit precisely into the legislative process in a timely manner. In AAUW's efforts in Illinois, while leadership on the national, state division and branch levels was supportive of ERA, many members found themselves in the position of combining home, family, career, church, educational and other interests with their desire to see ERA ratified in the state. The ERA Ratification Project came to be a means of bridging two shoals, by bringing together more effectively the volunteer efforts of many ERA enthusiasts within Illinois and throughout the nation.

In terms of political resources, such as marshalling expertise in the state's political process and establishing the reputation of the group for political action, AAUW's work in Illinois entailed a pioneering effort. To overcome the time constraints on many Illinois volunteers already engaged in letter writing, lobbying and other citizen-level activities, AAUW members from across the country volunteered to travel to Illinois to provide a "part-time, full-time" component to the ERA Ratification Project. Many AAUW Illinois volunteers took on greater responsibilities with the aid and assistance of out-of-state AAUW members, emphasizing that ERA is indeed a national political issue. The presence of volunteers for a prolonged period of time in the ERA Ratification Project Office not only added greatly to the *espirit de corps* of the coalition but served visibly as a reminder that coordinated multiple efforts can produce greater political clout than merely individual strategies.

AAUW, in its attempt to join forces with other groups in Illinois to gain political savvy, made a significant step forward in coalescing to achieve greater political impact, while still retaining its own identity. The focus in Illinois has been a wide educationally-oriented outreach program for AAUW's own membership and for the community, as well as a mobilization of informed and committed members to perform immediate political outreach activites.

To accomplish the latter requires further elaboration of still another of Ornstein's and Elder's criteria deemed vital to successful coalition efforts, namely, motivational resources: "If a group is composed of 'true believers' who are focused on their important issue or issues and who are committed to the cause, that intensity of feeling can multiply the group's influence far beyond its membership numbers."[39] Ironically, the seemingly exaggerated influence projected by anti-ERA groups underscores the veracity of this statement. Despite a constant stream of public opinion polls over the years revealing that a majority of the public support the ERA, limited, vocal and essentially right wing organizations have been successful to date in preventing some state legislatures from approving bicameral ratification of the ERA.[40] Creation of the new coalition ERA Ratification Projects where necessary challenges the success of the anti-ERA groups by implanting, in a central location, a wide variety of diverse organizations all devoting considerable attention of their own "true believers" to the cause of equal rights.

Additionally, "moral rectitude serves not only as a motivational force for group cohesion and activity, but it also provides a powerful line of argument to use in persuading public officials."[41] While anti-ERA groups have attacked the amendment on a variety of fronts arguably not associated with the spirit or intent of the ERA, its proponents remain motivated by the belief that equality of rights under the law secured by a contitutional amendment is an idea whose time has come. Such unshakable faith is an asset and significant in the efforts of the Illinois ERA Ratification Project.

Lastly, any consideration of the success of the ERA Ratification Project must take into consideration the presence of "intangible resources," such as the prestige of the organization attaching its name and commitment to a political issue and other influences which it might be able to bring to bear on the common goal sought by the coalition. As previously mentioned, AAUW brings with its participation a full century of tradition and dedication to the advancement of women. Moreover, realization that AAUW did not support the ERA in its inception in 1923 is indicative of the metamorphosis which the issue had undergone. AAUW members, personifying several decades of study and review of the ERA, concluded in 1971 that women's advancement in a more permanent and meaningful way could best be achieved through ratification of the ERA.[42] AAUW's own studies demonstrated that there had been change but no real progress in women's attempts to achieve legal parity with men.[43] Its participation in the ERA Ratification Project represents concrete recognition that AAUW is willing to devote whatever resources—tangible or intangible—it can muster to the attainment of an amendment granting women equality of rights under the law.

Conclusion

Since creation of the ERA Ratification Project in 1979, the Illinois House of Representatives defeated the ERA in 1980 by a vote of 102 to 71, once again a majority vote in favor, but falling five votes short of the 107 supermajority needed under the "Illinois Standard."[44] This disappointment, coupled with the election of Ronald Reagan, the first presidential nominee of the Republican Party since 1940 not to support the amendment, is of obvious concern to ERA proponents.[46]

The recent AAUW experience with coalition politics in the Illinois ERA Ratification Project suggests that large scale concerted action by like-minded groups is not necessarily sufficient in itself to insure victory in a single-issue political situation. Even so, the realization remains that the anti-ERA forces in Illinois also resorted to a genre of coalition politics, and in this respect, their efforts have been ostensibly more successful. One lesson to be drawn from the Illinois experience is that coalition politics can work and that through close coordination and collaboration of stategies, money, lobbying and purpose new legislative policies can be introduced and adopted. The problem, is the overt limitation of the time frame. Continual reassessment must be made of fluid political situations in each of the unratified states to determine the most feasible and expedient location to concentrate coalition strategies and energies.

The future of AAUW's coalition participation and the ERA in Illinois lies in the continuing resolution of three specific obstacles both within the Association and among the coalition members: 1) securing adequate financing; 2) attracting and maintaining dedicated leadership; and 3) promoting and garnering vigorous grassroots public support. If these critical needs can be met, then use of coalition politics is likely to produce beneficial results. To be sure, this is the challenge that AAUW and other supportive ERA organizations must confront as they reassess their ERA strategies in Illinois and in each of the unratified states in the aftermath of the November 1980 elections and upon the amendment period's expiration.

FOOTNOTES

1. Andrew M. Greeley, *Building Coalitions: American Politics in the 1970's* (New York: New Viewpoints, 1974), p. 130.

2. The classic work on political parties is V.O. Key, Jr., *Politics, Parties, and Pressure Groups* (4th ed.; New York: Thomas Y. Crowell, 1958). See especially Ch. 6, "Role and Techniques of Pressure Groups," pp. 142-77.

3. Greeley, Building Coalitions p. 132.

4. *Ibid.*

5. *Ibid.*

6. *Ibid.*

7. Detailed listings of groups and coalitions in support of the ERA can be found in Riane Tenenhaus Eisler, *The Equal Rights Handbook: What ERA Means to Your Life, Your Rights and the Future* (New York: Avon, 1978) pp. 141-51; Marguerite Rawalt, "The Equal Rights Amendment for Equal Rights Under the Law" (Washington, D.C.: Women's Equity Action League, 1976); and "Organizations Supporting ERA Extension," *National NOW Times*, September 1978.

8. Earl Latham, "The Group Basis of Politics: Notes for a Theory" in H.R. Manhood, ed. *Pressure Groups in American Politics* (New York: Charles Scribner's Sons, 1967), p. 21.

9. *Ibid.*

10. Ruth W. Tryon, *AAUW: 1881-1949* (Washington, D.C.: American Association of University Women, 1950), pp. 1,3; American Association of University Women, "AAUW, Is," August 1979; and American Association of University Women, *AAUW 1979 Charter and Bylaws* (Washington, D.C.: AAUW, 1979), especially p.4.

11. An excellent analysis of ERA's legislative history can be found in Barbara A. Brown, Thomas I. Emerson, Gail Galk and Ann E. Freedman, "The Equal Rights Amendment: A Constitutional Basis for Equal Rights for Women," *The Yale Law Journal*, 8 (April 1971), 981-85; For AAUW's early review of the ERA from a legislative policy perspective see *Journal of the American Association of University Women*, 18 (May 1925).

12. See "AAUW Is," col. 5.

13. Numerous studies have documented areas of legal discrimination against women. See generally U.S. Commission on Civil Rights, *Statement on the Equal Rights Amendment* (Washington, D.C.: Clearinghouse Publication 56, December 1978); Department of Health,

Education, and Welfare, *Report of the HEW Task Force on the Treatment of Women under Social Security* (Washington, D.C.: HEW, 1978); Citizens Advisory Council on the Status of *Women in 1975* (Washington, D.C.: Citizens Advisory Council on the Status of Women, U.S. Department of Labor, 1976); and Barbara Babcock, Ann Freedman, Eleanor Holmes Norton and Susan C. Ross, *Sex Discrimination and the Law* (New York: Little, Brown, 1975).

14. American Asociation of University Women, "Action for Equity" (Washington, D.C.: AAUW, 1980), col. 1.

15. "AAUW Is," especially col. 5, and American Assiciation of University Women, "Legislative Program and Resolutions 1979-81," (Washington, D.C.: AAUW, 1979)., cols. 1,3, and 7.

16. *Ibid.*

17. "Legislative Program and Resolutions 1979-81," cols. 1,3, and 7.

18. *AAUW 1979 Charter and Bylaws*, Article III, Use of Name, p. 4.

19. American Association of University Women Illinois State Division, *Directory and Bylaws 1979-80* (Elmhurst, Illinois: AAUW Illinois Division, 1979).

20. *Ibid.*, p. 1.

21. *Ibid.*, p. 112.

22. Report of the AAUW/ERA Ratification Task Force to the AAUW Board of Directors, February 8, 1980 (mimeograph); Minutes of the AAUW/ERA Ratification Task Force, January 8, 1980, and March 30, 1980 (mimeograph).

23. See "AAUW Is," col. 2; *AAUW 1979 Charter and Bylaws*, Article II, Purpose and Policy, pp. 3-4.

24. *AAUW Illinois State Division Directory and Bylaws*, pp. 13-14.

25. See Ellen Griffee, "ERA: How Extension Was Won," *Graduate Woman* January-February 1979, pp. 8-10; "No Time Limit for Equality," *The New York Times* June 22, 1978, cols. 1-6; p. 20. "Organizations Supporting ERA Extension," *National NOW Times*, September 1978; Eleanor Smeal, "For the ERA? Why an Extension," (Washington,D.C.: NOW Action Center, 1978); J Machlean, "Women Fight Back: ERA Extension," *Progressive* (February 1979), 43, cols. 38-40.

26. "AAUW Urges Congress to Extend ERA Ratification Deadline During Hearings," *Women Today*, May 29,1978, pp. 66-77.

27. Article 14, Section 4, "Amendments to the Constitution of the United States," Constitution of the State of Illinois, reprinted in Alan J. Dixon, *Handbook of Illinois Government* (Springfield: State of Illinois, 1979), p.100

28. House Rule 42, Illinois House of Representatives, Springfield, Illinois.

29. Illinois General Assembly votes on the equal rights amendment resolution:

> 1974 - Senate defeated by 6 votes; House by 12 votes
> 1975 - House passed; Senate defeated by 6 votes
> 1976 - Senate defeated by 7 votes
> 1977 - Senate defeated by 6 votes
> 1978 - House defeated by 2 votes
> 1979 - General Assembly adopted a rule that limits floor consideration of a constitutional amendment to only one per legislative session. The Senate and House also voted to retain the three-fifth's majority rule.
> 1980 - House defeated by 5 votes (102 in favor; 71 against)

Adapted from ERAmerica, "Status of ERA Ratification: 27th Amendment," July 1980.

It is interesting to note that Illinois already has a state equal rights amendment which reads: "The equal protection of the laws shall not be denied or abridged on account of sex by the State or its units of local government and school districts." The entire Constitution of the State of Illinois was adopted in Convention at Springfield on September 3, 1970 and ratified by the voters of the state on December 15, 1970. The provisions came into force on July 1, 1971. Constitution of the State of Illinois, Article 1, Section 18, reprinted in *Handbook of Illinois Government*, pp. 72, 74.

30. See "Thousands to Come to Chicago to National ERA March, May 10," *National NOW Times*, April 1980, pp. 1, 4, cols. 1-4.

31. "Action for Equity—What AAUW is Doing," *Graduate Woman* March/April 1980, pp. 15-17.

32. Norman J. Ornstein and Shirley Elder, *Interest Groups, Lobbying and Policymaking* (Washington, D.C.: Congressional Quarterly Press, 1978), p. 69. See also American Association of University Women, "Guidelines for AAUW Participation in Coalitions," in *AAUW Board Handbook on Policies and Procedures* (Washington, D.C.: AAUW, 1980).

33. Ornstein and Elder, *Interest Groups*, p. 70. A useful and practical analysis of the intricacies of network and coalition formation can be found in Peg Downey, "Multiplying Power: The Use of Networks and Coalitions," Washington, D.C.: Department of Education, 1980.

34. American Association of University Women, "Action for Equity: You Have a Part to Play," (Washington, D.C.: AAUW, January 1980); "Action for Equity Marches On," *Graduate Woman*, May/June 1980, pp. 48-49.

35. *Ibid.*

36. Mary A. Grefe, "A Question of Identity," *Graduate Woman*, November/December 1979, p. 41.

37. Ornstein and Elder, Interest Groups, p. 75.

38. See the July 1980 issue of *MS* Magazine devoted to "The Leadership Crisis," especially Charlotte Bunch, "Women Power: The Courage to Lead, the Strength to Follow, and the Sense to Know the Difference," *MS* July 1980, pp. 45-48, 95-97.

39. Ornstein and Elder, Interest Groups, p. 78.

40. A recent Harris poll commissioned by the National Federation of Business and Professional Women's Clubs, Inc. for ERAmerica showed that Americans favored ratification of the ERA 56% to 36%. Louis Harris and Associates, Inc., "Support for the Equal Rights Amendment: Nationwide Breakdown" (New York: Louis Harris and Associates, 1980); reprinted in *ERAmerica Report*, March 1980, p. 2. compare also to "public opinion polls by Gallup, majority of American voters favor ERA ratification," cited in *Women Today*, May 29, 1978, pp. 66-67. An analysis of the political implications and strategies of the opposition to the ERA can be found generally in Janet K. Boles, *The Politics of the Equal Rights Amendment, Conflict and the Decision Process* (New York: Longman, 1979).

41. Ornstein and Elder, *Interest Groups*, p. 78.

42. "AAUW Is," col. 5; American Association of University Women, "The AAUW Story" (Washington, D.C.: AAUW, 1978), cols. 4-5. See also generally Marion Talbot and Lois Rosenberry, *The History of the American Association of University Women, 1882-1931* (Boston: Houghton Mifflin, 1931), and Grefe, "A Question of Identity, p. 41.

43. Suzanne Howard, *But We Will Persist—A Comparative Research Report on the Status of Women in Academe* (Washington, D.C.: American Association of University Women, 1978); Betty Gordon Becton and Betty Belk Moorhead, *At Ease With ERA* (Washington, D.C.: American Association of University Women, 1979).

44. The vote came on June 18, 1980, prior to the June 30, 1980, adjournment of the Illinois General Assembly. Analysis of the vote is found in "Status of ERA Ratification," ERAmerica.

45. Warren Weaver, Jr., "Equal Rights Plan Splits Republicans Drafting Platform," *The New York Times*, July 8, 1980, p. 1, col. 3; p. B6, cols. 3-5.

THE EFFECT OF THE PRO- AND ANTI-ERA CAMPAIGN CONTRIBUTIONS ON THE ERA VOTING BEHAVIOR OF THE 80TH ILLINOIS HOUSE OF REPRESENTATIVES

Judson H. Jones

ABSTRACT. This study provides evidence that campaign financing has contributed to the defeat of the equal rights amendment (ERA) in Illinois. It is not the primary factor, but it is an important one. Since 1972 eleven votes have been taken on the ERA in the Illinois House and seven votes in the Senate. Also, since 1976, Illinois has required that the campaign finances of the candidates for state office be made public. both these developments provided a unique opportunity to study the effect over time of campaign contributions on the voting behavior of legislators with regard to a single "ideological" issue. The study focuses on the 80th House of Representatives. Six of the eleven House votes on the ERA were taken in its two sessions, two in 1977, and four in 1978. The law-makers fell into two important categories: consistent voters on this issue, and inconsistent ones. Using a multivariate analysis technique it was found that campaign donations considerably influenced the ERA positions of the inconsistent voters. it is assumed that ideology was primarily responsible for the consistent voters' positions. If this assumption is correct, then ideology is probably the primary influence on legislators' ERA voting behavior, Given its effect on the inconsistent voters, however, campaign financing must be considered an important factor in determining the outcome of the ERA in Illinois.

Introduction

In 1972 Congress presented for ratification the equal rights amendment (ERA) to the U.S. Constitution. The proposed amendment, which guarantees equality of rights before the law without regard to sex, passed both houses by wide margins: 354–23 in the House of Representatives on October 12,

Judson H. Jones is an Assistant Professor, in the Political Science Department of Southern Illinois University, Carbondale, IL 62901. The author is indebted to many of his friends and colleagues for their comments on an earlier version of this paper. He was especially indebted to Rose Jones, Joann Paine, John Baker and Roy Miller, all at Southern Illinois University at Carbondale. Also, he is grateful to Sarah Slavin, the editor of *Women & Politics*, and to two anonymous referees for their criticisms and suggestions, and wishes to thank Barbara Brown, Kevin Wright and Mark Smith for their cheerful and steady assistance in compiling the data.

1971, and 84–8 in the Senate on March 22, 1972. The resolution accompanying the proposed amendment included a seven-year deadline for ratification by three-fourths of the states, in this case thirty-eight. That deadline, March 22, 1979, passed with only thirty-five states having ratified the ERA, and three of those thirty-five have rescinded their ratification.[1] Before the seven-year deadline expired, however, supporters of the ERA lobbied to extend the time limit for ratification. On October 6, 1978, they won an important victory when the United States Senate approved a resolution which granted the states thirty-nine additional months to ratify the amendment.

Fifteen states either defeated the ERA or did not act on it. Supporters, in the face of heavy opposition from the Stop-ERA group, still hoped for ratification at the time this article was being prepared. They had to win three more states to ratify. A cursory examination of the states which did not pass the ERA led one to believe that their task was formidable. None of the Southern states except Texas passed the amendment. Nevada, Utah and Arizona did not approve it. Strong religious and conservative convictions were probably the obstacles in these states. The only industrialized state not to have passed the amendment is Illinois.

Illinois, except for Chicago, is highly rural and conservative in its outlook. Yet, Illinois was a logical target for the amendment's supporters. Even given the conservative nature of much of the state, a large industrial-liberal element favorable to the ERA resides in it. Also, the state has its own equivalent to the ERA. Article 1, Section 18, of the Illinois Constitution of 1970 states that: "The equal protection of the laws shall not be denied for abridged on account of sex by the State or its units of local government and school districts." In addition, both houses of the Assembly passed the ERA, although never simultaneously. The Senate passed the amendment in 1972, and the House passed it in 1975. Finally, many supporters believed that Missouri, another state which had not passed the ERA, was more likely to pass it if Illinois did.[2] Illinois, then, seemed to be a crucial state for the ERA supporters to win if the amendment was to be ratified. Thus, one of the primary battles between the forces for the ERA and those against it was in this state.

Research Design

This prolonged competiton between the pro- and anti-ERA forces for votes in the Illinois General Assembly together with the passage of a campaign funds disclosure law on September 3, 1974 provides a unique opportunity for studying the effect of campaign financing on the voting behavior of legislators on a single issue. Admittedly, the ERA is an ideological issue; one expects that a high proportion of legislators will consistently vote for or against the amendment depending upon their values. Yet, careful examination of the voting records on the ERA resolutions indicates that this issue is not an ideological one for a conspicuous proportion of the General Assembly's members. Many have changed their vote on the ERA one or more times, and at least one member has changed sides six times. One can surmise, therefore, that if a pro- or anti-ERA interest group provides these non-ideological assembly persons with sufficient "rewards" or "punishments," then their votes are likely to be delivered to the source of that reward or punishment. Campaign contributions are only one way to provide an incentive for a legislator to vote properly, but they are an important way.

It has long been assumed that candidates receiving substantial funding resources feel obligated to support policies beneficial to the groups providing those resources. There apparently have not yet been any studies which, using aggregate data, establish this link between campaign contributions and the voting behavior of legislators receiving those funds. The reason for this paucity of research has been the impossibility of obtaining the necessary information. But, since the passage of the Federal Election Campaign Act of 1971, and the new campaign finance laws enacted by forty-nine states between 1972 and 1976, this situation has changed drastically. A plethora of data now allows us to study this assumed relation more scientifically.

A serious problem in studying this relationship remains, however. Numerous variables affect legislators' votes. Since scientific experiments controlling for all effects on voting except for the receipt of campaign contributions cannot be performed on members of legislatures, the data available, despite their limitations, must be analyzed using multivariate techniques which allow inference of effects from the data. If campaign contributions cannot be consistently excluded as an explanatory variable of voting behavior, then eventually the conclusion that financing does indeed affect it must be made. This study, within the limitations of its data, provides evidence that campaign contributions do influence legislators' voting behavior even on an issue so ideologically "loaded" for many as the ERA.

Each state legislative candidate is required to submit three campaign finance reports to the Illinois State Board of Elections: a pre-election report, a post-election report and an annual report. In each report the candidate must disclose all aggregate figures concerning receipts and expenditures of his campaign finance committees, and itemize all receipts of $150 or more. All the available reports of the members of the 80th and 81st General Assemblies have been obtained. Specifically taken from these reports are the campaign finance data of the Stop-ERA political action committee and six pro-ERA political action committees: ERA Political Action Committee (ERA PAC), Illinois Women's Political Caucus, Women's Power Illinois Style, Chicago National Organization for Women Political Action Committee (Chicago NOW PAC), Committee for Passage of ERA and the National Women's Political Caucus.

At least one chamber of the Illinois legislature has voted on the ERA every year since 1972; however, campaign finance information in Illinois has been available only since 1976. This study is limited to the analysis of the ERA voting behavior of the representatives of the 80th Illinois General Assembly. The senators of that Assembly did not vote on the amendment, and all the ERA data on the 81st General Assembly were not available to us. Three pro-ERA groups, as of this writing, had not submitted their annual reports.

This focus on the 80th House of Representatives proves fortunate for two reasons. First, pro- and anti-ERA campaign financing escalated dramatically in 1978. Before then there was comparatively little funding by these groups, In 1976 the pro-ERA forces donated $1626 to eighteen winning candidates. Two-thirds of those donations were for fifty dollars or less. The anti-ERA forces donated nothing that year. In 1978 the pro- and anti-ERA organizations donated $31,340 and $37,695, respectively. Secondly, the 80th House voted six times on the ERA or related issues, two times in 1977 and four times in 1978. One hundred seventy-two members have complete voting records for these two time periods. Only five failed to finish their terms; therefore, there was little turnover and little change in the legislators between 1977 (time one) and 1978 (time two).

All the voting records on the ERA were obtained from the Equal Rights Amendment Ratification Project in Chicago. In this study there are two underlying dimensions to the measurement of voting behavior: direction and consistency. Each legislator's "direction" was determined by his/her position on his/her ERA vote: positive for a vote in favor of it, negative otherwise. Each legislator's "consistency" was determined by whether he/she switched sides on the issue over time. Thus, on the ERA there are: 1) consistently positive voters $(C+)$, 2) consistently negative voters $(C-)$, and 3) inconsistent voters. The inconsistent voters were divided further into two categories: 1) inconsistent voters whose last position in a time period was in favor of the ERA (I+), and 2) inconsistent voters whose last position was opposed to it (I−). There are, then four types of voters in each time period: C+, C−, I+ and I−. Votes in the Illinois General Assembly fall into five categories: yes, no, no vote, present and absent. since the ERA must obtain one hundred seven favorable votes to pass the House,[3] no, no vote, present and absent were treated as negative positions. The inclusion of absent in this category is based on interviews with many of the House staff, and the author's personal observations twice. This evidence overwhelmingly supports the conclusion that "absent" means the legislator had an opportunity to vote on the amendment but did not. Therefore, more measurement error would result by treating this category literally than by treating it as an unfavorable tally.

For each legislator the campaign contributions of the Stop-ERA group and the six pro-ERA groups, respectively, were summed. Excluding zeroes, these totals for Stop-ERA vary from $200 to $3000, while for the pro-ERA groups they vary from $15 to $11,000. Based on an examination of these distributions four arbitrary but relevant and useful categories were defined: 1) zero contributions, 2) contributions from $1 to $149, 3) contributions from $150 to $499 and 4) contributions of $500 or more (500+). Categories 2, 3 and 4 listed above were subdivided further into pro- and anti-ERA contributions, generating seven campaign finance categories in all.

A problem arose with five legislators included in this study; each received contributions from both sides. Stop-ERA outbid the pro-ERA forces in all five cases. The respective Stop- and pro-ERA contributions were: 1) $500, $15; 2) $600, $200; 3) $300, $100; 4) $300, $100; and 5) $500, $400. Given these figures, the pro-ERA contributions to these five individuals were ignored. At the risk of some error this simplified the analysis by eliminating a category, contributions from both sides. Justification for this action is founded on the relative figures. In each case but one Stop-ERA contributed substantially more dollars than did the anti-ERA groups.

During 1978, that is after time one but before the end of the time two period, 101 (59%) law-makers received campaign donations from pro- or anti-ERA groups, and 71 (41%) did not. This study's primary weakness is that the direction of causality is probably two-way; that is, campaign contributions cause voting behavior and voting behavior attracts contributions. Nevertheless, with a plausible assumption concerning causal direction, and with the legislators' time one voting patterns serving as a surrogate for a multitude of other factors, such as their party identifications, their district demographic properties, their educational backgrounds, their religious views and their ideologies, reasonable conclusions can be made about the effect of campaign contributions of the law-makers' voting behavior in time two.

Data Analysis

The data will be presented in four tables. These four tables are really sub-tables of one large arrangement, but to display the data in one such configuration would confuse rather than clarify. Table 1 exhibits the 1978 ERA voting behavior of the 1977 C+ voters together with their campaign receipts. Tables 2, 3 and 4 present corresponding data for the 1977 C− voters, the 1977 I+ voters and the 1977 I− voters.

In Table 1 it is evident that a considerable proportion of the 1977 C+

Table 1

Representatives of The 80th Illinois General
Assembly Who Voted Consistently In Favor of
ERA In 1977 with Their 1978 Pro- and
Anti-ERA Campaign Finance Receipts
and Their 1978 ERA Voting Behaviors

ERA Voting Behavior		ANTI-ERA RECEIPTS			PRO-ERA RECEIPTS				
1977	1978	500+	150-499	1-149	0	1-149	150-499	500+	
C+	C+				20 (68.97)	13 (72.22)	11 (91.67)	3 (100)	47 (74.60)
	C−	1 (100)							1 (1.59)
	I+				2 (6.90)	1 (5.56)	1 (8.33)		4 (6.35)
	I−				7 (24.14)	4 (22.22)			11 (17.46)
		1 (100)	0	0	29 (100.01)	18 (100)	12 (100)	3 (100)	63 (100)

C+ - Consistently in Favor of ERA
C− - Consistently in Opposition to ERA
I+ - Inconsistent Voting Behavior Ending in Favor of ERA
I− - Inconsistent Voting Behavior Ending in Opposition to ERA

voters were not sufficiently committed to the pro-ERA positon to remain firm in their support during 1978. Sixteen (25%) voted against the amendment at least once. Only four of these 16 finished the year in favor of it. One of the other twelve, with a large campaign donation from Stop-ERA, shifted his/her support to and voted consistently for the anti-ERA position.

Eighty-two % of those receiving campaign contributions from the pro-ERA groups persisted in their constant support of the amendment. In contrast, only 69 percent receiving no donations did so. Also, the proportions of steadily loyal supporters increased as the monetary value of the donations increased. Seventy-two % of those receiving from $1 to $149, 92% of those receiving from $150 to $499; and 100% of those receiving $500 or more remained consistent supporters. Perhaps campaign funding made a difference even to the representatives who were ideologically inclined to favor the ERA.

From Table 2 it is apparent that a high proportion (85%) of the 1977 C – voters remained C – in 1978. This proportion of anti-ERA partisans is higher than the corresponding proportion (75%) of the pro-ERA loyalists in Table 1. The pro-ERA forces contributed to the campaigns of three 1977 C – voters. One of these representatives switched sides completely; one voted inconsistently but finished 1978, once again, anti-ERA, and one remained steadily opposed to the amendment in spite of the donation. Of those receiving no contributions 67% remained loyal C – voters. This figure is little different from the corresponding pro-ERA figure in Table 1: 69%. As with the 1977 pro-ERA supporters in Table 1, Table 2 illustrates that medium to large contributions correspond with high levels of constancy on the part of anti-ERA loyalists; 100% of those receiving from $150 to $499 remained constantly opposed to ERA, and 95% of those receiving $500 or more remained so opposed.

Table 3 shows that 25 (66%) of the 1977 I+ voters remained inconsistent in their 1978 voting habits, but 24 of the 25 finished the year opposing the ERA. Twenty-six % became 1978 C+ partisans, while only eight % became 1978 C – supporters. The voting patterns corresponding to the campaign finance patterns in Table 3 present a confusing picture. Only three of 14 representatives (21%) financed by the pro-ERA forces became 1978 C+ supporters. This figure compares unfavorably with the law-makers receiving no contributions. Thirty-one % of them became 1978 C+ voters. The anti-ERA forces fared better; 60% of their finance targets became 1978 C – supporters. An explanation for this phenomenon could be that Stop-ERA awarded, on the average, larger donations than the pro-ERA groups. The pro-ERA donations of from $1 to $149 appear to have been remarkably unsuccessful in attracting supporters. However, a serious problem with this explanation is that the pro-ERA 500+ donations were even more unsuc-

Table 2

Representatives of The 80th Illinois
General Assembly Who Voted Consistently in
Opposition to ERA in 1977 with Their 1978
Pro- and Anti-ERA Campaign Finance Receipts
and Their 1978 ERA Voting Behaviors

ERA Voting Behavior		ANTI-ERA RECEIPTS				PRO-ERA RECEIPTS			
1977	1978	500+	150-499	1-149	0	1-149	150-499	500+	
	C+				1 (4.76)	1 (50)			2 (2.99)
C-	C-	20 (95.24)	22 (100)		14 (66.67)		1 (100)		57 (85.07)
	I+	1 (4.76)			2 (9.52)				3 (4.48)
	I-				4 (19.05)	1 (50)			5 (7.46)
		21 (100)	22 (100)	0	21 (100)	2 (100)	1 (100)	0	67 (100)

C + - Consistently in Favor of ERA
C - - Consistently in Opposition to ERA
I + - Inconsistent Voting Behavior Ending in Favor of ERA
I - - Inconsistent Voting Behavior Ending in Opposition to ERA

cessful. It is obvious from Table 3 that there are strong factors affecting voting behavior which cannot be easily overcome with campaign contributions.

The salient information conveyed by Table 4 is that there were only four 1977 I− voters. Two received no contributions and remained inconsistent voters in 1978; one of these finished the year in favor of the amendment, and one finished opposed to it. The pro-ERA forces once again fared rather badly with their one contribution. The representative on whom they bestowed their largess remained an inconsistent voter, finishing the year against their position. In contrast, the one 1977 I− voter receiving a Stop-ERA donation became a loyal 1978 C− voter. However, since the number in this table is so small, nothing more can be said about it.

Entropy analysis was used to analyze the complex composite table formed from Tables 1, 2, 3, and 4.[4] Table 5 gives the results. Although the focus of this analysis will be on the proportion of the dependent variable's distribution affected by the independent variables, an explanation of the other effects and the disorder is expedient. The degree of order influenced by the distribution of the dependent variable itself is a result of uncontrolled exogenous variables affecting the outcome in a non-random manner. The categories chosen to measure the dependent variable also can affect this figure. To illustrate, in this study if it had been decided to collapse the I+ and I− voters into one category, the result for this effect in Table 5 would have been 0.0031 instead of 0.111. In effect, this alternative choice of standard would have hidden the exogenous influences on the inconsistent voters discovered by using the gauge adopted. To speculate, some plausible fac-

Table 3

Representatives of The 80th Illinois
General Assembly Who Voted Inconsistently
on ERA but Ended in Favor of It
in 1977 with Their 1978 Pro- and
Anti-ERA Campaign Finance Receipts
and Their 1978 ERA Voting Behaviors

ERA Voting Behavior		ANTI-ERA RECEIPTS				PRO-ERA RECEIPTS			
1977	1978	500+	150-499	1-149	0	1-149	150-499	500+	
I+	C+		1 (25)		6 (31.58)	2 (20)	1 (50)		10 (26.32)
	C-	1 (100)	2 (50)						3 (7.89)
	I+						1 (50)		1 (2.63)
	I-		1 (25)		13 (68.42)	8 (80)		2 (100)	24 (63.16)
		1 (100)	4 (100)	0	19 (100)	10 (100)	2 (100)	2 (100)	38 (100)

C+ - Consistently in Favor of ERA
C- - Consistently Opposed to ERA
I+ - Inconsistent Voting Behavior Ending in Favor of ERA
I- - Inconsistent Voting Behavior Ending in Opposition to ERA

Table 4

Representatives of The 80th Illinois
General Assembly Who Voted Inconsistently
on ERA but Ended In Opposition to It In
1977 with Their 1978 Pro- and Anti-ERA
Campaign Finance Receipts and Their
1978 ERA Voting Behaviors

ERA Voting Behavior		ANTI-ERA RECEIPTS				PRO-ERA RECEIPTS			
1977	1978	500+	150-499	1-149	0	1-149	150-499	500+	
	C+								0 (0.00)
I-	C-		1 (100)						1 (25)
	I+				1 (50)				1 (25)
	I-				1 (50)		1 (100)		2 (50)
		0	1 (100)	0	2 (100)	0	1 (100)	0	4 (100)

C+ - Consistently In Favor of ERA
C- - Consistently In Opposition to ERA
I+ - Inconsistent Voting Behavior Ending In Favor of ERA
I- - Inconsistent Voting Behavior Ending in Opposition to ERA

tors which might be causing these exogenous effects are the legislators' vote bargaining habits and their social interactions; however, further study is necessary to isolate them. The proportion of disorder is determined by two factors: random behavior and exogenous forces collectively affecting the dependent variable randomly. The degree of disorder possibly can be reduced if additional variables affecting voting could be included in further study, but, due to random behavior, this item can probably never be eliminated entirely.

Table 5 signified that the two independent variables together determine approximately 51% of the distribution of the 1978 ERA voting behavior. Previous voting behavior is the most important indicator, affecting almost 36% of the distribution. Campaign contributions are not as powerful, but their influence, which exceeds 15% of the House's ERA voting distribution, is not unimportant. This degree of effect can be crucial in close roll calls, the rule rather than the exception in the Illinois General Assembly ERA votes. In the total picture, however, there are other variables probably more influential than campaign financing. If ideology is the dominant factor underlying consistent voting, then it is the strongest influence. Tables 1 and 2 documented strong propensities for the 1977 consistent voters on either side to remain so.

Eliminating the 1977 consistent voters from the investigation, and analyzing only the 1977 inconsistent voters, reinforces this conclusion, and at the

TABLE 5

Results of Entropy Analysis on
Tables 1, 2, 3, and 4; the 1977
C_+, C_-, I_+ and I_- Voters

Sources Affecting Order on the Dependent Variable	Proportion of the Dependent Variable's Distribution Affected
Distribution of the Dependent Variable	
1. 1978 ERA Voting Behavior	0.111
Independent Variables (Sources of Explanatory Power)	
1. 1977 ERA Voting Behavior	0.357
2. 1978 Campaign Contributions	0.152
Total Explanatory Power	0.509
Total Proportion of Order	0.620
Proportion of Disorder	0.380
Total	1.000

same time shows where campaign donations have their strongest effect. Table 6 depicts this information.

Examining Table 6 reveals that the two independent variables determine 32% of this group's 1978 ERA voting distribution. This figure compares unfavorably with the 51% effect on the distribution of all the 80th House members. Campaign contributions, however, have considerable influence on these inconsistent voters. Over 27% of their 1978 voting distribution is influenced by donations. As one would expect, their previous inconsistent voting behavior indicates little about their 1978 ERA voting behavior. The consistent voters, therefore, are causing the large effect depicted in Table 5 on the 1978 ERA voting distribution. Campaign funding, however, is conspicuously effective on the inconsistent voters. This is no insignificant finding when one considers that over 24% of the House voted inconsistently in 1977, and nearly 30% voted inconsistently in 1978.

TABLE 6

Results of Entropy Analysis on
Tables 3 and 4; the 1977 I_+
and I_- Voters

Sources Affecting Order on the Dependent Variable	Proportion of the Dependent Variable's Distribution Affected
Distribution of the Dependent Variable	
1. 1978 ERA Voting Behavior	0.273
Independent Variables (Sources of Explanatory Power)	
1. 1977 ERA Voting Behavior	0.043
2. 1978 Campaign Contributions	0.275
Total Explanatory Power	0.318
Total Proportion of Order	0.591
Proportion of Disorder	0.409
Total	1.000

Conclusions

Three developments in American politics make these findings important: 1) the increasing propensity for legislators to make a "career" of politics; 2) the decline of party influence in elections; and 3) the increasing cost of campaigns. Kwang Shin and John Jackson show that the turnover in state legislatures is generally decreasing.[5] Illinois, specifically, does not fit this description; but its turnover rates have been consistently low since 1931. Only the houses of representatives in three states, California, New York and Virginia, have average turnover rates lower than Illinois's 27.9%. The mean turnover rate for the houses of representatives in all states since the 1930s is 45%.[6] Illinois, then, is one of the leading states in this development. It seems that its House members like their jobs and wish to keep them. The decline of party influence in Illinois elections is documented well. In a recent study David Everson and Joan Parker find that:

> . . .the evidence suggests that fewer Illinoisans pull the straight party lever in the voting booth; more voters call themselves independents, ignore traditional party organizations and pay more attention to candidates' stands on single issues than to broad-based party platforms.[7]

The Congressional Quarterly reported the cost of the U.S. House elections had risen 34% over and above the increase in the Consumer Price Index between 1972 and 1978.[8] Presumably, Illinois legislators have not escaped this increasing cost of campaigns. This study recorded earlier the increased donations of the pro- and anti-ERA forces from 1976 to 1978. While studies by this author documenting campaign expenditures in Illinois are forthcoming, a cursory examination of the data confirms that expenditures are increasing.

Taken together, these three developments are encouraging law-makers to become "political entrepreneurs." They must organize and pay for their elections, relying less and less on party support. Campaign contributions under these conditions become more and more valuable and necessary for elections and re-election. Those who donate, however, are not philanthropists; they surely want some influence in return. In the meantime the decline of party support in elections means the decline of party influence on policy, creating a power vacuum between the law-maker and his contributors. The logic is compelling. If this trend persists, eventually interest groups through campaign financing will capture large policy areas, if they have not already done so. Well-meaning legislators will not be able to stop this development either. If they sufficiently resist interest group influence, opponents will be found to replace them.

This study found that campaign financing did influence legislators' voting behavior even on an ideological issue such as the ERA. It was not the primary influence, but, nevertheless, it had its effect. Given this finding, the probability that the ERA will pass the Illinois General Assembly is small. In order to reverse the previous outcomes the pro-ERA forces would have had to elect more ideologues favorable to their cause, or sway more non-ideologues. Since donations do not always succeed in buying votes, the first strategy is a necessary one. Campaign funding, however, is a necessary element of both strategies. The problem is that contributions cut both ways. The anti-ERA forces are at least as politically adept as the pro-ERA groups, and their track record in the Illinois General Assembly is excellent.[9]

FOOTNOTES

1. For a study on whether a state may rescind its ratification see Samuel Freedman and Pamela Naughton, *ERA: May a State Change Its Vote?* (Detroit: Wayne State University Press, 1978).

2. I am indebted to Sarah Slavin, who was a coordinator of the ratification coalition in Missouri in 1972 and 1973, for this information. Ms. Slavin is presently the editor of *Women & Politics.*

3. In 1972 the Illinois General Assembly acted under the rule that an amendment to the Constitution must obtain a favorable vote from a majority of the elected members. The next year, to be consistent with the 1970 constitution of the State of Illinois, it was ruled that the ERA would require an affirmative vote of 3/5 of those elected, 36 in the Senate and 107 in the House. This ruling was challenged in the federal courts. On February 19, 1975, the final federal court ruling said that the Illinois Constitutin could not impose a 3/5 requirement for ratification of amendments to the U.S. Constitution, but that each General Assembly is free to decide which majority it wishes to set. Motions requiring a 3/5 vote for ratification were soon passed in both houses. That is the way the situation stands at this writing.

4. The entropy analytical technique used in this study was introduced to the political science discipline by R. Darcy and Hans Aigner, "The Uses of Entropy in the Multivariate Analysis of Categorical Variables," *American Journal of Political Science,* 24 (February 1980), pp. 154-174. In Appendix 1 a discussion and demonstration of the model are provided.

5. Kwang S. Shin and John S. Jackson, III, "Membership Turnover in U.S. State Legislatures": 1931-1976," *Legislative Studies Quarterly,*" 4:1 (1979), pp. 95-104.

6. *Ibid.,* pp. 97-99.

7. David H. Everson and Joan A. Parker, "Ticket Splitting: An Ominous Sign of Party Weakness," in *Illinois Elections: Parties, Patterns, Reapportionment, Consolidation,* ed. Caroline A. Gherardini, et al. (Springfield, Illinois: Sangamon State University Publication, 1979), p. 56-59.

8. *Congressional Quarterly, Weekly Report,* September 29, 1979, p. 2151.

9. For an anecdotal and perceptual account of the effect of campaign contributions on the ERA voting behavior of the members of the Illinois House of Representatives see: Barbara Brotman, "The ERA battle of the bankrolls," *Chicago Tribune,* November 2, 1980, Section 12, p. 1. As one would expect there are cases described where contributions are said to have had little, if any, influence; however, there is ample evidence presented which supports the conclusion that financing, especially that from Stop ERA, affected the ERA positions of many

legislators. To cite one example, John Matijevich (D., North Chicago) the House ERA spon sor in 1980 is quoted as saying, "Legislators couldn't say pro-ERA forces were strongly behind them, but they could say Stop ERA was. Stop ERA was giving large amounts to many more candidates; pro-ERA groups seemed to highlight two or three districts."

APPENDIX 1

A Demonstration of Entropy Analysis

Entropy analysis is the technique adopted in this paper to analyze the data. Entropy can be defined in many ways, but perhaps its best definition for social scientists is "disorder" or "randomness." Perfect entropy would mean total randomness or complete disorder. Zero entropy would mean perfect order.

The technique is an important and useful contribution to the discipline. Its primary value in this study is measuring the explanatory power of combinations of categorical independent variables on a dependent one. The method is easy to use and interpret, and "makes no assumptions whatsoever concerning the numeric properties of the variables, the nature of their distributions, or the nature of their interrelationships" (Darcy and Aigner, "The Uses of Entropy," p. 171). The interested reader should consult Darcy's and Aigner's article, but an illustration of their model's behavior is illustrated in Table 7.

Example one of Table 7 exhibits total randomness or disorder. The univariate and conditional distributions of the dependent variable are uniform; therefore, there is no evidence of constraint on the dependent variable or of explanatory power by the independent variable. The entropy analysis reflects this; the proportion of disorder is one. Example two illustrates some constraint, 0.28, in the distribution of the dependent variable, but no explanatory power by the independent variable. The degree of constraint is a function of the non-uniformity, or order, in the distribution of the dependent variable itself. This order could be the result of exogenous variables or measurement decisions. The conditional distributions of the dependent variable are proportionally identical. This accounts for the lack of explanatory power of the independent variable. Example three portrays a perfect relationship between the variables. The univariate distribution of the dependent variable is uniform, but its conditional distributions are perfectly ordered; therefore, 100% of the dependent variable's distribution is accounted for and explained by the independent variable. The proportion of disorder in this example is zero.

.   TABLE 7

Three Bivariate Distributions Contrived
to Illustrate the Behavior of
Entropy Analysis

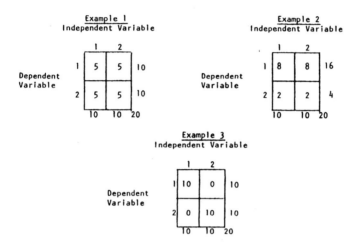

Sources Affecting Order on the Dependent Variable	Proportion of the Dependent Variable's Distribution Affected		
	Ex. 1	Ex. 2	Ex. 3
Distribution of the Dependent Variable	0.00	0.28	0.00
Independent Variable (Source of Explanatory Power)	0.00	0.00	1.00
Total Proportion of Order	0.00	0.28	1.00
Proportion of Disorder	1.00	0.72	0.00
Total	1.00	1.00	1.00

These bivariate examples were used for the sake of simplicity only. Entropy analysis is not confined to the investigation of bivariate distributions; it has considerably more flexibility. Like analysis of variance and regression analysis it can be used, as it is in this study, to analyze functions with "m" number of independent variables and one dependent one. In fact, it can be used to examine the relationship between "m" independent variables and "n" dependent ones. Given its flexibility and the paucity of assumptions needed to use it properly, this author expects the model will be used extensively in the social sciences.

BIBLIOGRAPHY

CURRENT RESEARCH ON WOMEN AND POLITICS: JOURNAL ARTICLES

Susan Gluck Mezey

ALLEN, W. "Family Roles, Occupational Statuses, and Achievement Orientations among Black Women in the United States," *Signs*, 4 (Summer 1979), 670-94.

As members of two minority groups, black women represent excellent subjects for research into the dynamics of discrimination, motivation and occupational achievement. Despite the established tradition of black female labor force participation, black women workers represent a relatively neglected research topic. Many questions remain concerning the attitudes, motivations, roles and statuses of black women in the labor force. This paper contributes to a clarification of these questions through a comparative analysis of occupational status and achievement orientation among black women. Specifically, census and survey data are employed to investigate differences in the occupational status of black women relative to white females and males of both races. Achievement orientations among black women are then compared with those of the other sex-race groupings in order to ascertain whether the measured differences in internalized attitude, value or belief sets seem to substantiate observed occupational status differences.

Susan Gluck Mezey is affiliated with the Political Science Department, DePaul University, 2323 N. Seminary Ave., Chicago, IL 60614.

BAHR, S. "The Effects of Welfare on Marital Stability and Remarriage," *Journal of Marriage and the Family*, 41 (August 1979), 553-60.

The purpose of this study was to estimate the effects of welfare on marital dissolution and remarriage. The data were from a sample of 4,322 females age 30-44 from the National Longitudinal Surveys. It was found that those who received AFDC, food stamps or other public assistance dissolved their marriages more frequently than those not receiving welfare. This finding held among low-income whites but not among low-income blacks. By controlling for other relevant variables, it was revealed that the relationship between welfare and marital dissolution decreased somewhat as duration of marriage increased. The remarriage rate of divorced females was three times greater among non-AFDC than AFDC recipients. This occurred among both low-income blacks and low-income whites. However, as age increased, the relationship between AFDC and remarriage dissolved.

BEAR, S., M. BERGER and L. WRIGHT. "Even Cowboys Sing the Blues: Difficulties Experienced by Men Trying to Adopt Nontraditional Sex Roles and How Clinicians Can Be Helpful to Them," *Sex Roles*, 5 (April 1979), 191-98.

Difficulties clinicians experience in appropriately treating men attempting to adopt nontraditional sex roles are discussed and suggestions made to ameliorate these difficulties. While the impact of the women's movement has made therapists more sensitive to societal influences on the behavior of women, comparable attention has not been paid to societal influences on the sex-role stereotypical behavior or to the price paid by men who violate stereotypical sex-role expectations. Further, clinicians who have been socialized into dominant societal values may have difficulty tolerating men who are trying to abandon higher status "traditional masculine" values for nontraditional ones; such clinicians are unlikely to provide decent treatment for males espousing new sex roles.

BIANCHI, S., and R. FARLEY. "Racial Differences in Family Living Arrangements and Economic Well-Being: An Analysis of Recent Trends," *Journal of Marriage and the Family*, 41 (August 1979), 537-51.

Among both races, recently there has been a shift away from traditional living arrangements. Changes have been more significant among blacks and, thus, racial differences are now greater than at the time of the Moynihan Report (1965). The economic consequences are described by analyzing trends in per capita income for types of families. Income has risen in all types of families, but the improvements are greater in husband-wife families. Among both races, the gap which separates the economic well-being of those in husband-wife families from those in families headed by a woman has widened. A declining proportion of children and adults live in families with the greatest per capita income and an increasing fraction live in families with the lowest income. Changes in living arrangements are related to family welfare policies.

BRADBURY, K., S. DANZIGER, E. SMOLENSKY and P. SMOLENSKY. "Public Assistance, Female Headship, and Economic Well-Being," *Journal of Marriage and the Family*, 41 (August 1979), 519-35.

In recent years there has been a rapid growth in the number of households headed by women and in the proportion of these households receiving public assistance. This paper presents a model to test the hypothesis that changes in the public assistance system contributed to the increase in these households. Current Population Survey data on the number of women in various household status categories and the level of economic well-being associated with these categories are analyzed. Major findings include: 1) most of the increase in female-headed households was accounted for by childless women who are generally ineligible for public assistance benefits; 2) although the public assistance system has become more generous in recent years, a married woman who becomes a female head can expect a substantial drop in her level of economic well-being.

BURSTEIN, P. "Equal Employment Opportunity Legislation and the Income of Women and Nonwhites," *American Sociological Review*, 44 (June 1979), 367-91.

This article examines the impact of federal employment opportunity legislation on the income of white women, nonwhite women and nonwhite men relative to the income of men at the national level since the late 1940s. The analysis differs from those previously published in comparing all groups with white men, including changes in attitudes in the analysis, and dealing in detail with enforcement of the laws. The model developed in the article works well when used to examine increases in nonwhite income, but does not deal satisfactorily with the incomes of white women. The findings indicate that there are important differences between race and sex discrimination which will have to be taken into account in theories of labor market discrimination.

CAMP, R. "Women and Political Leadership in Mexico: A Comparative Study of Female and Male Political Elites," *Journal of Politics*, 41 (May 1979), 417–41.

The existing information on the political role of women comes mostly from political cultures with predominantly English or West European groups, and women in political leadership of the more traditional developing countries have received very little attention. The paper provides information on the role of women as leaders in Mexican politics. Such a study, in general terms, might suggest what role, if any, women can play in changing government policies once they reach leadership positions. Mexico is a useful country to examine because it represents the stereotype of masculine supremacy, social cleavages and authoritarian politics predominant in many countries. The paper concludes by speculating that women would contribute little to changing the political system in Mexico because, like men, in order to achieve success, they have accepted the informal rules of the dominant political culture.

CARROLL, B. "Political Science, Part I: American Politics and Political Behavior," *Signs*, 5 (Winter 1979), 289–306.

If it seemed in 1974 that the women's movement had introduced the potential for changes in the way political science studies women and in the way it defines political activity, five years later there is little evidence that this potential has been realized. This is not to deny that works of significance have appeared in the intervening years. There has been a substantial expansion of published writings on women. Although the number of books has been small, over eighty-five articles were published between 1976 and 1978 in over forty scholarly journals or serials. Of these, nearly fifty articles have appeared in eighteen major journals of political science, social science, public administration or political theory in the United States. Seven journals (including two foreign ones) published special issues or groups of articles on women. Less encouraging is the fact that many journals published only one relevant article, and the American Political Science Review published no article specifically on women in the three-year period.

CARVER, J. "Women in Florida," *Journal of Politics*, 41 (August 1979), 941-55.

In Florida the traditional attitudes that have limited women's options are being challenged. The movement to Florida of large numbers of non- southerners, has made Florida somewhat different from its sister states of the South. The influx of newcomers has resulted in the formation of two cultures with respect to women: a conservative culture in the northern part of the state, where native southerners are most numerous and old attitudes strongest, and a culture more receptive to change in the central and southern parts of the state. It is the Floridians in this latter area who have taken the lead in opening opportunities for women.

CLARKE, H., and A. KORNBERG. "Moving Up the Political Escalator: Women Party Officials in the United States and Canada," *Journal of Politics*, 41 (May 1979), 442-77.

This study examines two explanations that have been offered concerning the participation, or lack of it, of women in politics. These explanations are: the unequal statuses and resources that men and women bring into politics; the socialization of men into political roles and the socialization of women into culturally approved wife-mother roles. These explanations are used to inform and to organize this study of the political recruitment and careers of men and women party officials in four metropolitan areas in the United States and Canada. Of particular concern in this paper is an attempt to explain variations in the placement of men and women in the several parties into three organizational categories that are termed "elites," "insiders" and "stalwarts."

CONSTANTINOPLE, A. "Sex-Role Acquisition: In Search of the Elephant," *Sex Roles*, 5 (April 1979), 121-33.

Social learning and cognitive-developmental theories of sex-role acquisition have yet to receive clear and unequivocal research support. While it is apparent that sex typing of interests and behaviors does occur in early childhood, we are at a loss to explain the mechanisms involved. A model of sex roles as rules is presented, which attempts to analyze the acquisition of sex roles as similar to the process of pattern recognition in vision and speech. Social-learning theory can help to account for how the child acquires the distinctive features of sex-role patterns, while cognitive-developmental theory points to the categories that are essential in this process.

CORCORAN, M. "The Economic Consequences of Marital Dissolution for Women in the Middle Years," *Sex Roles*, 5 (June 1979), 343-54.

This article uses longitudinal data from the Panel Study of Income Dynamics to explore how changes in marital status affect the economic status of married women in their middle years. Results demonstrate that when a marriage ends, the economic status of women declines considerably. Components of income change are discussed, with emphasis on the extent to which women can compensate for the loss of a spouse's income through increases in paid labor, by changes in living arrangements and by the use of public and private transfers.

DOMINICK, J. "The Portrayal of Women in Prime Time, 1953-1977," *Sex Roles*, 5 (August 1979), 405-11.

A content analysis of 1,314 television programs and 2,444 starring characters appearing on prime-time television from 1953 to 1977 revealed that the number of females in starring roles has remained relatively constant over the last 25 years and that most women are still found in situation comedies. While the number of women shown as housewives or housekeepers has declined from the 1950s to the present, the makeup of the television labor force has consistently shown no relationship to the real-life employment patterns of women. The data seem to support the findings announced in a recent study by the U.S. Commission on Civil Rights, which concluded that women were underrepresented on television and were frequently seen in stereotyped roles.

DUNCAN, O. "Indicators of Sex Typing: Traditional and Egalitarian, Situational and Ideological Responses," *American Journal of Sociology*, 85 (September 1979), 251-60.

A new latent class model yields estimates of the prevalence of ideological and situational responses by Detroit mothers to four questions on assignment of household chores to boys and girls. In 1953 there was virtually no ideological traditionalism (although the modal response pattern was the most traditional one) but a significant number of ideologically egalitarian responses. Both kinds of ideological response had become more frequent by 1971. By 1976 the modal response was the ideologically egalitarian one, as the entire response distribution had shifted toward the egalitarian pole. Yet the highest ratio of ideological to situational responses was observed among the consistently traditional respondents. The trend in ideological traditionalism suggests that the ideological justifications for traditional definitions of sex roles develop as a reaction to the emergence and promulgation of egalitarian ideologies.

ENGLAND, P. "Women and Occupational Prestige: A Case of Vacuous Sex Equality," *Signs*, 5 (Winter 1979), 252–65.

The women's movement has prompted questions about women's share of the rewards from occupational roles. This paper examines the amount of occupational prestige accorded to women in the United States and concludes that when interest focuses solely on occupational prestige, there is a surprising lack of discrimination against women. On their face, these findings contradict notions of extreme sexism in the labor market. Yet, this sex equality of prestige is rather vacuous. Although women have a very similar occupational prestige distribution to that of men, women's incomes are vastly lower than men's, and women seldom have the power to supervise or otherwise control a man's work. Sex equality of prestige is surprising in light of women's lesser income and power because, in general, there is a correlation between the prestige, income and interpersonal power associated with occupation.

ERICKSEN, J., W. YANCEY and E. ERICKSEN. "The Division of Family Roles," *Journal of Marriage and the Family*, 41 (May 1979), 301–13.

This paper analyzes the marital role division between 1,212 couples taken from a probability sample of the Philadelphia urban area. It concentrates on the division of household tasks, of child care and of paid employment. Using log linear techniques, it examines the effects of a variety of variables measuring social networks and the relative status of husband and wife. Data show support for a marital power model with husband's income negatively related to shared roles and with wife's education positively related to shared roles. Black couples are more likely to share household tasks than white couples.

FELDBERG, R., and E.N. GLENN. "Male and Female: Job Versus Gender Models in the Sociology of Work," *Social Problems*, 26 (June 1979), 524–38.

Work has been seen as the central social process that links individuals to industrial society and to each other. Although work issues are considered universal, the actual study of work has proceeded along sex-differentiated lines so that: 1) women are rarely studied as workers; 2) studies that do include women offer biased interpretations; and 3) the entire analysis of work is distorted. It is argued that these problems arise from the use of the sex-segregated models of analysis: the job model for men and the gender model for women. Further it is argued that these models lead researchers to ask different kinds of questions according to the sex of the workers, to treat men as uniform in relation to family and women as uniform in relation to employment and, implicitly, to use the patterns of men's relation to employment as the standard in analysis. The paper suggests that work should be reconceptualized to include forms of unpaid as well as paid work and to incorporate gender stratification into the analysis of work.

FERBER, M., and J. HUBER. "Husbands, Wives, and Careers," *Journal of Marriage and the Family*, 41 (May 1979), 315–25.

This research examines the extent to which spouse's level of education hinders or helps the careers of Ph.D. recipients. Using multiple regression to analyze data obtained from 1,053 persons who received their Ph.D.'s from 1958 to 1963 and 1967 to 1971, it was found that having a Ph.D. spouse negatively affected wives' labor-force participation and also husband's offices held and articles published; there was no direct effect on earnings for either sex. For both husbands and wives, marriage to a highly educated spouse has at least some negative career effects.

FLORA, C. "Change in Women's Status in Women's Magazine Fiction: Differences by Social Class," *Social Problems*, 26 (June 1979), 558–69.

Women's magazines reflect and reinforce ideal characteristics of different social groups. Comparing the images of women in women's magazine fiction between 1970 and 1975 and between middle-class and working-class magazines, the former reflected economic and political movements in the relative status of women of that class. Middle-class women's fiction portrayed women as less likely to be valued for dependence and ineffectuality in 1975 as compared to 1970, and more likely to be valued for independence; plot devices were less likely to rely on traditional stereotypical female modes of behavior. In contrast, female passivity became more valued in working-class fiction. While in 1970, working-class women's fiction portrayed and valued the more active female characteristics, by 1975, that fiction had become significantly more traditional than middle-class fiction.

FOWLKES, D., J. PERKINS and S.T. RINEHART. "Gender Roles and Party Roles," *American Political Science Review*, 73 (September 1979), 772-81.

This article used discriminant analysis to assess sex and party differences across four aspects of party organization: incentives for participation, party role definitions, party activities and electoral ambition. The results illustrate that gender roles operate most distinctly in the two areas of electoral ambition and party activities. Party context is more important than sex in terms of the other two areas, party-role definitions and incentives for participation. The authors conclude that party activists' gender-related behavior can be better understood by discovering how the context of party organization either modifies or reinforces such behavior.

GEISE, L.A. "The Female Role in Middle Class Women's Magazines from 1955 to 1976: A Content Analysis of Nonfiction Selections," *Sex Roles*, 5 (February 1979), 51-62.

One hundred sixty nonfiction articles and features from Ladies' Home Journal and Redbook were systematically selected and examined for their projections of the female role between 1955 and 1976. Changes found in both magazines, and particularly in Redbook which directs itself toward younger women, paralleled a number of important societal changes. Attitudes toward female employment were found to have undergone changes during this period, as presented in magazine selections. At the same time, however, a rejection of traditional sex roles appeared decidedly less popular than a flexible consideration of nontraditional alternatives. The image of women as narrow creatures, interested only in home and family, was not supported even during the earlier years in this sample.

GELB, J., and PALLEY, M.L. "Women and Interest Group Politics: A Comparative Analysis of Federal Decision-Making," *Journal of Politics*, 41 (May 1979), 362-92.

The authors consider the extent to which emergent feminist groups have been successful in influencing the American policy-making system. The kinds of issues most likely to foster additional successes and the techniques most useful in achieving political goals are surveyed. In this latter context, the Equal Credit Opportunity Act of 1974, the anti-sex discrimination provisions of Title IX of the Education Amendments of 1972, the anti-abortion Hyde Amendments of both 1976 and 1977, and the Amendment to Title VII of the Civil Rights Act of 1964 ending the discrimination in employment based upon pregnancy are examined. The authors contend that success is more easily attained if issues are perceived as dealing with role equity rather than with role change for women.

GERTZOG, I. "Changing Patterns of Female Recruitment to the U.S. House of Representatives," *Legislative Studies Quarterly*, 4 (August 1979), 429-45.

A systematic examination of the backgrounds of women who were elected to the House between 1916 and 1976 reveals that a sharply decreasing proportion were widows of congressmen who died in office. There was also a discernible decrease in the percentage of congresswomen whose families possessed either extraordinary wealth or a history of political activity. In the meantime, there was a significant increase in the proportion of female House members who had legal training, who had elective experience and who had a living spouse at the time of their initial election. A decrease in the average age of congresswomen was also reported. These findings suggest that the resources once found useful by female House candidates are no longer relied upon as fully as they once were and that the proportion of American women who have access to the effective political opportunity structure and who are available for public office has increased. Both of these developments have important implications for a democratic political system.

GHAFFARADLI-DOTY, P., and E. CARLSON. "Consistency in Attitude and Behavior of Women with a Liberated Attitude Toward the Rights and Roles of Women," *Sex Roles*, 5 (August 1979), 395-404.

This study was designed to determine the extent of consistency of attitude and behavior of women with liberated attitudes toward their rights and roles, and to identify determinants of inconsistency between attitude and behavior. The Attitude Towards Women Scale, Rotter's Locus of Control Scale, the Ego-Strength Scale, the Self-Esteem Scale, the Liberated Behavior Questionnaire, and the Attitude of Family and Friends Questionnaire were administered to 242 women. Women with more liberated attitudes tended to act more liberated. Also, women with liberated attitudes tended to act more liberated if their close friends were liberated and if they themselves were more aware of leaders in the women's liberation movement. The personality measures did not relate to the tendency to act liberated.

GOVE, W., and M. HUGHES. ''Possible Causes of the Apparent Sex Differences in Physical Health: An Empirical Investigation,'' *American Sociological Review*, 44 (February 1979), 126–46.

For the past fifty years it has been consistently reported that men have higher rates of mortality, while women have higher rates of morbidity. The higher rates of mortality for males can be largely explained by the fact that they have higher rates for the chronic diseases which are the leading causes of death. The explanation of why women have higher rates of morbidity, however, remains unanswered. Recent literature suggests three possible explanations: 1) a greater willingness among women as compared with men to report they are ill and/or to react overtly to an illness; 2) the greater ability of women to adopt the sick role due to their lack of obligations; and 3) the possibility that the reported differences reflect real sex differences in illness. This paper evaluates these explanations and provides support for the view that the sex differences in morbidity are real. The data analyzed show that when one controls for marital status, living arrangements, psychiatric symptoms and nurturant role obligations, the health differences between men and women disappear.

HACKER, S. ''Sex Stratification, Technology and Organizational Change: A Longitudinal Case Study of AT&T,'' *Social Problems*, 26 (June 1979), 539–57.

Recent technological displacement in AT&T affected workers differently by sex. This paper addresses several questions: the tendency of organizational research to ignore the critical variable, sex, in the study of change; questions of sex, race and class in technological displacement; and the role of women as a reserve labor army. The conclusions reached were the following: technological displacement affected both management and nonmanagement women; affirmative action placed more men in traditionally women's work than the reverse; observations of sex stratification in families and unions suggest that analysis of the linkages between home and work roles is crucial in understanding problems of a divided work force; and, women did appear to serve as a reserve army during the period of technological change.

HAYLER, B. "Abortion," *Signs*, 5 (Winter 1979), 307-24.

Since the 1973 Supreme Court decisions declaring it a constitutional right, abortion has become the most common surgical procedure in the country. More than one million abortions were performed in 1977, and it has been estimated that one American woman in four will have an abortion sometime during her life. However, strong disagreements remain over the extent of the right to abortion and its consequences. This essay reviews the major legal cases affecting abortion rights since 1973 and discusses research on: 1) the history of abortion and birth control in America; 2) the abortion reform movement of the 1960s and the antiabortion movement of the 1970s; 3) the decision to abort and its physical and mental health consequences; 4) issues of race and class; and 5) feminist theory on abortion.

HEDLUND, R., P. FREEMAN, K. HAMM and R. STEIN. "The Electability of Women Candidates: The Effects of Sex Role Stereotypes," *Journal of Politics*, 41 (May 1979), 513-24.

This study analyzes three explanations usually given for the relative absence of female office holders: personality differences, situational factors and sex role socialization. The latter is usually divided into two distinct explanations: a lack of interest on the part of women, and low support from others for their participation. Data collected during a survey of Milwaukee County residents in late 1976 were used to study these explanations. The questions asked about likely voting behavior in local elections where women had been candidates and were likely to be candidates in upcoming elections. The data show that most respondents' votes would not be affected by the sex of the candidate. However, the type of public position had an important impact on support levels. The study concludes by indicating that sex-role stereotyping seems to take place among high participation voters. Questions must be raised, however, about the effects of political socialization experiences on differing voting behavior responses to candidates described in sex-role stereotype terms.

HOFFERTH, S. "Day Care in the Next Decade: 1980-1990," *Journal of Marriage and the Family*, 41 (August 1979), 649-58.

Over the next decade the growth in the number of preschool children with working mothers is expected to be rapid, both because of the increase in the total number of children and because more of children's mothers will be employed. This raises an important concern, since the supply of individual day care providers appears to be shrinking at the same time that the need for such care is increasing. Most evidence points to increased parental dependence on group care, not only for their 3–5 years old, but also for infants and toddlers. Demographic, economic and attitudinal factors, as well as public policy, have contributed to this trend and can be expected to play a major part in the future demand for and supply of day care.

HOFFERTH, S., and K. MOORE. "Early Childbearing and Later Economic Well-Being," *American Sociological Review*, 44 (October 1979), 784-815.

Early childbearing has been assumed to result in numerous social and economic problems, including school drop-out, large families and poverty. However, few studies have been conducted within a multivariate, nonrecursive framework; and researchers have not traced the casual and cumulative effects of an early first birth. Using data from the National Longitudinal Surveys of young women on a subsample of women who have borne a child by age 27, strong direct effects are found to indicate that later childbearers complete more education, have smaller families and work fewer hours at age 27. The relationship with education is recursive among women having a first child by age 18, but simultaneous among later childbearers. Effects of age at first birth on economic well-being at 27 are indirect. Having an early first birth was found to be less detrimental to the later economic well-being of black women than of white women.

HOLLAND, J., and C. OGLESBY. "Women in Sport: The Synthesis Begins," *Annals of the American Academy of Political and Social Sciences*, 445 (September 1979), 80-90.

Sports have emerged as a primary area of controversy about men's and women's roles. The authors argue that women's sport has changed dramatically in recent years while men's sport has changed little. An additional level of change in sport, synthesizing elements of the traditional men's and women's sport experience would be socially beneficial. Essential elements of play, game, sport and athletics are identified as defined in the emerging sport sciences. Selective socialization of males and females via sport was accomplished through the shaping of "masculine" and "feminine" sport experiences. The effect of the women's movement has been to adopt traditional sport as instrumentality, rather than masculinity training. This requires little restructuring of sport by men. A new conception of sport is presented in which the elements of traditional men's and women's sport are theoretically synthesized. Because of the past emphasis on the masculine-instrumental elements of sport, it is hypothesized that a temporal focus on the feminine-expressive elements is necessary to the occurrence of a synthesis.

HOLLY, S. "Women in Management of Weeklies," *Journalism Quarterly*, 56 (Winter 1979), 810-15.

Relative opportunities for men and women in journalism appear to vary within different sectors. The weekly newspaper has been shown to offer more opportunities to women than some other areas. This study attempts to clarify whether women do have better opportunities with weekly newspapers than with larger metropolitan dailies. It attempts to determine whether women journalists nonetheless have a lower status than men in this specific sector of journalism. The findings show that women were generally less well paid than men, have less control over newspapers than men, are not as likely to hold management positions than men. Despite these differences, opportunities are still better for women on weekly newspapers than on dailies.

JACOBSON, W. "A Rose by Any Other Name: Attitudes Toward Feminism as a Function of Its Label," *Sex Roles*, 5 (June 1979), 365-71.

Male and female subjects were asked to rate one of the following labels on a variety of evaluative dimensions: "equal rights for women" (ERW), "feminism" (FEM), "women's liberation" (WLN) and "women's lib" (WLB). It was found that there were differences among the labels, with ERW being the most positively evaluated and WLN being the most negatively evaluated. Women generally were more positive on evaluations.

KAMERMAN, S. "Work and Family in Industrialized Societies," *Signs*, 4 (Summer 1979), 632-50.

The separation of work and home—or work life and family life—has been identified as one of the most significant characteristics of industrialized societies. This paper analyzes the development of separation of work and family in five European countries (France, West Germany, East Germany, Sweden and Hungary) that has led to various public policy initiatives and how this development is viewed in each country. The dominant pattern in these countries is to establish special policies for working women. In these countries, the assumptions are that women have primary responsibility for childbearing and child care, and because essential supplementary help is needed for only a brief period of time, it will not be too expensive. The countries that have taken this position make the implicit assumption that the dichotomy between work and family is a problem for women only.

KARNIG, A., and S. WELCH. "Sex and Ethnic Differences in Municipal Representation," *Social Science Quarterly*, 60 (December 1979), 465-81.

This study has the following aims: 1) to examine and compare the level of municipal government representation of Anglos, blacks and Mexican-American males and females; 2) to ascertain whether the correlates of equitable representation, including minority population, government structure and minority resources, are similar for both minority males and females; and 3) to determine whether a substantial degree of inter-minority competition exists; that is, whether the rate of representation obtained by one minority-gender group comes at the expense of other minorities or, conversely, generally acts only to reduce the representation of Anglo males. Results show that women are less well represented than men, and that minority women are the most poorly represented. Anglos obtained more posts than their numbers would justify but only because of Anglo males.

KATZ, P. "The Development of Female Identity," *Sex Roles*, 5 (April 1979), 155–78.

People may be described and categorized along many dimensions, but few dimensions seem to be as salient as gender. Gender-role socialization begins at birth and continues throughout life. This paper, which assumes that the development of sex roles begins in infancy and continues throughout life, suggests that there are three overlapping but distinctive developmental levels of sex roles. These levels include: 1) learning what is appropriate behavior for a male or female child, 2) acquiring concepts about what is appropriate as a potential female or male adult, and 3) behaving in ways that are deemed appropriate for male and female adults across the life span. The model proposes that each level has stages in which different tasks are to be acquired.

LAMB, C. "Equal Employment Opportunity and the Carter Administration: An Analysis of Reorganization Options," *Policy Studies Journal*, 8 (Winter 1979), 377–83.

Responding to his 1976 campaign pledge, President Carter has reorganized the federal government's enforcement of equal employment opportunity (EEO) laws. He has done so by shifting some EEO responsibilities from the Civil Service Commission and the Department of Labor to create a "Super-EEOC." This article examines why President Carter chose the EEO reorganization that he did from the standpoint of advantages and disadvantages. Also presented are alternative reform options that the President could have selected, that would have involved increasing EEO coordination or reorganization. Such coordination organization would have entailed new legislation that would have gone far beyond the creation of a "Super-EEOC."

MACKE, A., G. BOHRNSTEDT and I. BERNSTEIN. "Housewives' Self-Esteem and Their Husbands' Success: The Myth of Vicarious Involvement," *Journal of Marriage and the Family*, 41 (February 1979), 51–57.

This study tests the common assertion that women, especially upper middle-class housewives, vicariously experience their husbands' success. These findings (for 121 mostly upper middle-class housewives) contest that assertion. Husbands' success does positively affect a housewife's self-esteem, but only indirectly, through its effect on perceived marital success. Only husband's income has a direct positive effect on self-esteem, while other successes of the husband actually lower self-esteem. These findings, made more dramatic by a comparison with professional married women for whom none of the above effects appear, demonstrate the ambiguous impact traditional marriage has on women. Since marriage is traditionally a basis for a woman's identity, successful marriage increases her feelings of worth. However, the specific role arrangements may reduce her feelings of personal competence.

MARGOLIS, D.R. "The Invisible Hands: Sex Roles and the Division of Labor in Two Local Political Parties," *Social Problems*, 26 (February 1979), 314–24.

This is a study of the division of labor between men and women in the Democratic and Republican party organizations of a small New England town. Interviews, observations and logs kept by the town committee members revealed a difference in styles of performance that made men stand out more than women. Women's political activities more often took place in settings where they could not be seen, and the roles played by women were typically those without title or acknowledgement, while men usually held highly visible leadership positions. A similarity was observed between sex-linked roles and behavior patterns based in the family, and the parts played in the political arena. Because of these differences women often were unnoticed and unrewarded, although they worked more than twice as many hours on political activities as did men during the study period. Also, women logged more than three times as many separate political interactions as men.

MAHONEY, E.R., and J.G. RICHARDSON. "Perceived Social Status of Husbands and Wives: The Effects of Labor Force Participation and Occupational Prestige," *Sociology and Social Research*, 63 (January 1979), 364–74.

The perception of the general social status of husbands and wives as a function of their respective achieved and derived occupational statuses was examined experimentally. Varying occupational statuses of married women are compared to the housewife status as the means to assess the relative contribution of labor force involvement to her and her husband's general social status. The results indicate that it is the husband's occupational status which alone is the determinant of both his and his wife's general social status, with the wife's occupational status having no effect. These results are discussed in relation to critiques of male determined stratification models and to research on the effects of working wives upon family social status.

McCALL, D.K. "Simone de Beauvoir, *The Second Sex*, and Jean-Paul," *Signs*, 5 (Winter 1979), 209–23.

Published in 1949, when feminism was no longer and not yet a live issue, *Le Deuxieme Sexe* has come to be accepted as a pioneering and uniquely ambitious attempt to explore, within a philosophical framework, all aspects of women's situations. The primacy of Beauvoir's contribution, however, seems to be undermined by the pervasive influence in *The Second Sex* of Sartre and of Sartrean existentialism, a philosophy which in the context of feminist theory is perceived as ideologically sexist. In this essay, the author attempts to develop these antagonistic claims and to mediate between them. The purpose of the mediation is to subvert both the domestication of *The Second Sex* as a generally "unread" classic and the dismissal of it as merely an imitation of Sartre, thereby hoping to revive the problematic status of Beauvoir's text and open it for further feminist analysis.

MILLER, J., SCHOOLER, C., KOHN, M. and MILLER, K. "Women and Work: The Psychological Effects of Occupational Conditions," *American Journal of Sociology*, 85 (July 1979), 66–94.

For employed women, job conditions that encourage self-direction are related to effective intellectual functioning and an open, flexible orientation to others, while those that constrain opportunities for self-direction are related to ineffective intellectual functioning and a rigid social orientation. Moreover, several types of job pressures and uncertainties are related to less effective intellectual functioning, unfavorable evaluations of self or a rigid social orientation. Causal analysis demonstrates that job conditions not only correlate with but actually affect psychological functioning. For women, as for men, occupational conditions have a decided psychological impact.

NORTON, M.B. "American History," *Signs*, 5 (Winter 1979), 324–27.

Students of women's history have dramatically advanced the understanding of their own field in the years since 1975. Special issues of journals, volumes composed of original essays and book-length studies attest to the vitality of current scholarship. This essay concentrates on articles on the assumption that the most important recent books have been reviewed elsewhere and that articles represent the cutting edge of scholarly production. The major publications of the past four years may be grouped into three, distinct categories: amplification and modification of themes identified previously; detailed investigations into aspects of 19th and 20th century women; and significant breakthroughs into the study of colonial women. Each of these is discussed in this review essay.

O'KELLY, C. "The Impact of Equal Employment Legislation on Women's Earnings: Limitations of Legislative Solutions to Discrimination in the Economy," *American Journal of Economics and Sociology,* 38 (October 1979), 419–30.

Although a strong legal basis now exists for equal opportunity in employment for women, women's earnings have actually dropped relative to men's. This holds true even when experience on the job, life-time work experience and education are similar. Females are also still twice as likely as males to be below the poverty line. The impact of low female earnings may be of even greater significance today, because of the increase in female-headed families. Equal opportunity legislation has not been sufficient to end economic sexism.

OKIN, S.M. "Rousseau's Natural Woman," *Journal of Politics,* 41 (May 1979), 393–416.

Rousseau's ideas and arguments about women—their nature, their education and their proper place in the social and political order—are worthy of thorough examination for two important reasons. First, women are a "non-issue" in many of the great works of political philosophy; and Rousseau is one of the very few major philosophers who had a considerable amount to say about women and their place in society. Second, Rousseau's arguments and conclusions about women exemplify very clearly the way that political philosophers, insofar as they have referred to the subject, have tended to argue about the female half of the human race. The paper specifies and explains those aspects of Rousseau's writings about women which exemplify the general patriarchal bias of political theory.

PENG, S., and J. JAFFE. "Women Who Enter Male-Dominated Fields of Study in Higher Education," *American Educational Research Journal*, 16 (Summer 1979), 285-93.

Using data drawn from the National Longitudinal Study of the High School Class of 1972, this study examines 16 variables, classified into categories of family background, high school experience, academic ability, life-goal orientations and extent of education planned, that might influence women's entry into male-dominated fields of study in higher education. Results indicate that women in male-dominated fields have higher academic ability and more course work in science and mathematics in high school, and that they are more work-oriented than women in traditional fields. Results also indicate that family influence on women's entry into male-dominated fields is not significant.

PINES, A. "The Influence of Goals on People's Perceptions of a Competent Woman," *Sex Roles*, 5 (February 1979), 71-76.

Traditional and profeminist males and females were shown one of two videotapes of a competent woman who planned either to pursue her career or to stay home with her family. Results indicate that: 1) the woman was perceived as more able when she planned to pursue her career; 2) females' perceptions were more positive in the Career condition and males in the Family condition; 3) females' perceptions to the stimulus person were consistent with their attitudes, while males' perceptions were not.

POSNER, J. "It's All in Your Head: Feminist and Medical Models of Menopause (Strange Bedfellows)," *Sex Roles*, 5 (April 1979), 179-90.

The purpose of this article is two fold. First, it addresses the substantive area of menopause. It argues that there has been and continues to be a paucity of literature on the topic, which may be largely due to the stigma associated with aging females in our society. Though some current women's studies literature has addressed itself to this area, the few studies that have emerged from the recent wave of feminist research have tended to perpetuate aspects of the medical model of menopause, i.e., it's all in your head. This ironic compatibility between medical establishment and feminist models of menopause is the second focus of the article.

RAKOWSKI, S., and J. FARROW. "Sex-Role Identification and Goal Orientation in Teenage Females," *Psychological Reports*, 44 (April 1979), 363-66.

This research examines the relationship between sex-role stereotyping and career goals of young women from a junior high and high school. Questionnaires administered include measures of attitudes toward women, careers and goal orientation. Although most subjects (n = 57 of 91) chose careers within traditional sex-typed areas, there were differences between both career and sex-role attitudes of junior high and high school females who selected nontraditional careers.

ROBINSON, D. "Two Movements in Pursuit of Equal Employment Opportunity," *Signs*, 4 (Spring 1979), 413-33.

The Civil Rights Act of 1964 is a landmark of American law. Title VII of the act dealt with equal employment opportunity and was significant for two reasons: it was the first attempt at the federal level to outlaw discrimination by employers and trade unions; and it extended its protections to women as well as blacks. Title VII thus represented the hopes of two great modern movements of social change: the civil rights movement and the feminist movement. This paper discusses the enactment of Title VII and the ensuing struggle over its implementation during its first decade of existence.

ROSENBACH, W., R. DAILEY and C. MORGAN. "Perceptions of Job Characteristics and Affective Work Outcomes for Women and Men," *Sex Roles*, 5 (June 1979), 267-78.

One hundred twenty-three men and women participated in a study designed to assess their attitudes about job dimensions and affective work outcomes. This study found that very few differences existed between women's and men's perceptions of job dimensions and work outcomes. It was also shown that little difference existed between men's and women's perceptions of positive relationships between job dimension and affected work outcomes. The authors conclude that existing differences work attitudes are artifacts of hierarchical position and sex-role stereotyping and will disappear when women are allowed to move into jobs that are characterized by the presence of high levels of intrinsic job dimensions.

SALAMON, S., and A.M. KEIM. "Land Ownership and Women's Power in a Midwestern Farming Community," *Journal of Marriage and the Family*, 41 (February 1979), 109-19.

Control over land, a scarce resource for farmers, is found to be the source of women's power in a community of central Illinois farm families. Data were obtained mainly from interviews with and participant observation of 22 households of German extraction. Because men control the actual farming and distribution of what is produced, women generally cede power obtained by means of land ownership to husbands or male relatives. This shift of authority and other agricultural practices in rural America are seen to account for male domination in both family and community. Women appear to make a trade-off of lower status and less power for male management of the family enterprise which assures them a financially secure widowhood.

SAVELL, J., J. WOELFEL, B. COLLINS and P. BENTLER. "A Study of Male and Female Soldiers' Beliefs About the Appropriateness of Various Jobs for Women in the Army," *Sex Roles*, 5 (February 1979), 41-50.

The purpose of this paper is to document the often discussed and recently initiated expansion of women's role in the U.S. Army and to present evidence regarding one aspect of soldiers' probable reaction to this expansion—viz., the extent to which soldiers believe certain military jobs are appropriate for women and, in particular, the extent to which these beliefs are related to respondent sex, rank and expectation of leaving the Army before retirement. The data show that respondents express generally favorable attitudes towards the idea of employing women in traditionally male jobs with the exception of women as rifle-carrying infantry soldiers. The authors conclude by raising questions about the validity of these data and possible interpretations of the results.

SHABAD, G., and K. ANDERSEN. "Candidate Evaluations by Men and Women," *Public Opinion Quarterly*, 43 (Spring 1979), 18-35.

A widely accepted generalization in the social science literature is that women tend to personalize politics and politicians. The purpose of this article is two fold. The first is to determine whether an analysis of the available U.S.

survey data from 1952 to 1976 tends to support the claims made about how women differ from men in their assessments of politicians. The second is to suggest alternative and more precise ways of conceptualizing both men's and women's responses to the evaluations of political leaders.

SHANLEY, M.L. "Marriage Contract and Social Contract in Seventeenth Century English Political Thought," *Western Political Quarterly*, 32 (March 1979), 79-91.

One of the most striking instances of the extension of the conceptual revolution of the seventeenth century was the change which took place in the conceptualization of the marriage contract. Much of the change in thinking about the basis of the marriage relationship was provoked or inspired by the political debates of both the Civil War and the Restoration. The royalists thought they had found in the marriage contract a perfect analogue to any supposed contract between the king and his subjects, for marriage was a contract but was in its essence both hierarchical and irrevocable. Parliamentarian and republican writers were forced to debate the royalist conception of marriage as well as of kingship. The theoretical arguments which emerged from these debates over political sovereignty eventually became the bases for Liberal arguments about female equality and marriage.

SIGEL, R., and J. REYNOLDS. "Generational Differences and the Women's Movement," *Political Science Quarterly*, 94 (Winter 1979), 635-48.

This article examines the dispositions toward the contemporary women's movement and its goals of two generations of similarly educated women. Specifically, it is a comparison of mothers and daughters who have attended (or are attending) the same college. Two competing hypotheses are offered to explain the basis of support. One hypothesis identifies the social position of women as the key variable, starting with the assumption that all women occupy similar positions in the social structure, the stratum theory. The other hypothesis focuses on age-based differences in experiences and socialization patterns and their consequences for the movement, the generational hypothesis.

STAUDT, K. "Class and Sex in the Politics of Women Farmers," *Journal of Politics*, 41 (May 1979), 492-512.

The data from this case study indicate that there is a good deal of differentiation among women which has resulted from economic and political change. Patterns of agricultural service delivery have differential effects on the sexes, particularly among nonelite farmers. The most neglected clientele of the agricultural administration, nonelite women have bonded together to compensate for that discrimination. Elite women farmers experience equity in agricultural service delivery, and that equity reinforces both differentiation among women and the privileged position of the emerging elite class.

TANGRI, S., and G. STRASBURG. "Can Research on Women Be More Effective in Shaping Policy?" *Psychology of Women Quarterly*, 3 (Summer 1979), 321-43.

This paper examines ways in which researchers could enhance the policy relevance of their research and ways in which the psychology establishment could encourage the development of policy-relevant research. It also describes the large array of roles and settings for social scientists in the federal policy structure. Important policy issues affecting women are presented and discussed; particularly, the relation between female solidarity and community support systems is shown as an illustration of how an area of research can be made more useful.

TEDROW, L., and E.R. MAHONEY. "Trends in Attitudes Toward Abortion: 1972-1976," *Public Opinion Quarterly*, 43 (Summer 1979), 181-89.

Trends in attitudes toward abortion are examined over the 1972-1976 period. While an overall tendency of more liberal attitudes is noted, important differences over time are apparent by gender, education, occupational prestige and religiosity.

THORNTON, A., and D. FREEDMAN. "Changes in the Sex Role Attitudes of Women, 1962-1977: Evidence from a Panel Study," *American Sociological Review*, 44 (October 1979), 831-42.

This paper documents a tremendous shift women have made toward more egalitarian sex role attitudes between 1962 and 1977. The shift toward egalitarianism was considerably more pronounced for the global items concerned with general principles of role segregation and division of authority within the home, than for more specific aspects of role specialization, such as sharing of housework or the legitimacy of non-home activities for mothers. In 1962 sex role attitudes bore no appreciable relation to a wide spectrum of individual characteristics. By 1977 many of these basic characteristics were related to sex role attitudes. The experience of the women during the 1962 to 1977 intersurvey period also was associated with a shift in sex role attitudes.

TOPOL, P., and M. REZNIKOFF. "Achievers and Underachievers: A Comparative Study of Fear of Success, Education and Career Goals, and Conception of Woman's Role Among High School Senior Girls," *Sex Roles*, 5 (February 1979), 85-92.

Two groups of 16 high school senior girls, achievers and underachievers, were compared on the following variables: educational and career goals, conception of woman's role and fear of success (FOS). There were significant differences between groups with regard to their goals. In contrast to underachievers, achievers also had a more contemporary view of the roles women should assume in society.

VAN VELSOR, E., and L. BEEGHLEY. "The Process of Class Identification Among Employed Married Women: A Replication and Reanalysis," *Journal of Marriage and the Family*, 41 (November 1979), 771-78.

Until recently, the study of stratification dealt mainly with social processes among men. Recent research on class identification has focused on women, with varying results. This paper replicates two conflicting studies of class identification among married women. It is found that: 1) an employed married woman uses a combination of her own, her husband's and her father's characteristics in assessing her own status; and 2) an unemployed married woman borrows status from her husband. These data suggest that when a revised model for married working women is used, neither race nor mother's characteristics are significant indicators of an employed wife's class identification.

WELCH, S., and A. KARNIG. "Correlates of Female Office Holding in City Politics," *Journal of Politics*, 41 (May 1979), 478–91.

Focusing on city councils and mayoral seats in 264 U.S. cities over 25,000, this research explores some determinants of female membership in local offices and updates knowledge of the level of female representation in city councils. The primary concern is with variables measuring political structures and environments; but several key demographic features in each city are also explored.

WAX, R. "Gender and Age in Fieldwork and Fieldwork Education: No Good Thing Is Done by Any Man Alone," *Social Problems*, 26 (June 1979), 509–22.

With examples chosen principally from her own fieldwork, the author shows how age and gender affect the conduct of field research facilitating the study of some groups and inhibiting (or prohibiting) the study of others. Because much instruction about fieldwork ignores age and gender, it leaves the novice ill-prepared to cope with the vicissitudes of actual research. Further, it has led to inaccurate portraits of societies marked by sexual segregation. Male fieldworkers often believe they have described the totality, when in fact their ethnographic vision has been restricted to half or less. In many cases, mature women have the greatest scope as fieldworkers.

WOLF, W., and N. FLIGSTEIN. "Sex and Authority in the Workplace: The Causes of Sexual Inequality," *American Sociological Review*, 44 (April 1979), 235–52.

This paper contributes to our understanding of the causes of the restriction of women from positions of authority in the workplace. It ascertains the extent to which the sex gap in aspects of authority can be explained by the following three factors: 1) women's qualifications, 2) the behaviors and policies of employers, and 3) the attitudes and behaviors of women themselves. While the amount of sex difference in aspects of authority that can be explained by women's qualifications is substantial, it is not the most important factor responsible for the restriction of women from positions of authority. Further, strong evidence is presented that suggests the behaviors and policies of employers are much more important causes of sexual differences in authority in the workplace than are the attitudes and behaviors of the women themselves.

ZIMMERMAN, S., P. MATTESSICH and R. LEIK. "Legislators' Attitudes Toward Family Policy," *Journal of Marriage and the Family*, 41 (August 1979), 507-17.

Although many have advocated the need for a comprehensive family policy for the United States, the concept remains ambiguous. This exploratory research surveyed legislators in Minnesota about their attitudes toward family policy and the goals and areas of activity they perceived as being most appropriate to it. Of the 13 variables examined for their potential effects on legislators' attitudes toward family policy, family life cycle stage emerged as having the strongest influence. The findings indicate a need for broad public discussion about family policy so that family policy maps of legislators may be more clearly drawn and, hence, prospects of a coherent family policy more likely.

THE ROPER CENTER

Robert Darcy
Cheryl Handley

*The Machine Readable Archives Division
of the National Archives and Records Service*

While this section of *Women & Politics* is concerned primarily with data from academic research, scholars need to be aware that other sources of data are also available. Today, probably the largest source of machine-readable data is the United States government. Millions of tapes containing a great variety of data have already been generated or commissioned by the government, and additional data bases are continually being created. Many of these have little long-term interest, but many do offer great potential for scholarly exploration. It is the task of the Machine-Readable Archives Division of the National Archives and Records Service to ascertain which data needs to be preserved for future use and which can be destroyed once its original purpose has been served. It is also the task of the Machine-Readable Archives Division to prepare the data for, and make it available to, the public. Although the need for careful processing and the preparation of documentation has limited the number of studies currently available to under one thousand, the number of data bases now housed by the Machine-Readable Archives Division is quite large. In 1981 the *Catalog of Machine-Readable Records in the National Archives of the United States* will be published, facilitating the academic use of these data.

Robert Darcy is with the Political Science Department at Oklahoma State University, Stillwater, OK 74078. Cheryl Handley is affiliated with The Roper Center, University of Connecticut, U- 164R, Storr, CT 06268.

115

Availability

The National Archives charges $65 for each full tape ordered. Although extracting needed data can reduce the total cost for large multi-reel data sets, additional costs can occur should users wish to have the Archives extract portions of data sets. There is also a cost of 15¢ per page for copying documentation, a cost that increases to 20¢ if only partial documentation is desired. Again, partial documentation can often satisfy the needs of the researcher while reducing costs to the researcher. The Machine-Readable Archives Division welcomes inquiries from scholars concerning data bases. Inquiries, letters and phone calls, should be directed to: Machine-Readable Archives Division (NNR), National Archives and Records Service, Washington, D.C. 20408, (202) 724-1080.

A large number of the National Archive's data bases contain a sex variable or data on women. Many of these, however, contain only a few variables or are otherwise not of primary interest to those of us in women's studies. Ross Cameron, archivist at the Machine-Readable Archives Division, went through the available data bases and selected a number which should interest scholars in our field. While space prevents publishing all of them now, a selection is reproduced below.

THE AMERICAN SOLDIER IN WORLD WAR II: LEISURE TIME AC-TIVITIES 1943–1945 [File Number: 3-330-80-1 (F)] Army Research Institute.

A sample of 25,177 representative of a cross-section of black and white male soldiers and white WAC personnel stationed in the U.S. and Europe, 1943–1945. Variables include information on leisure-time activities provided for soldiers by the Army, the USO, the Red Cross and local communities. Activities include atheltics, radio programs, movies, newspapers, shows and dances. Theatre of operations, home-state and camp location is also coded.

DATA FORM: Logical Record

REFERENCE: Samuel A. Stouffer and others, *Studies In Social Psychology in World War II*. 4 Volumes, (Princeton: Princeton University Press, 1949–50).

DATA STATUS: Available

CONTACT: Machine-Readable Archives Division, National Archives and Records Service.

THE AMERICAN SOLDIER IN WORLD WAR II: TREATMENT OF WOMEN IN THE ARMY: 1945 [File Number 3-330-80-1 (A)] Army Research Institute.

A total of 7,502 Army nurses and WACs was sampled at bases in the U.S., the South Pacific and the Burma-India Theater. Variables include attitudes of female military personnel toward the overall treatment, condition and use of women in the Army, attitudes toward job assignments, regulations affecting women, the importance of women to the war effort, equality of treatment for men and women, social life in the Army, leisure-time facilities for women and opportunities for advancement. Plans for post-war education, occupation and marital plans are included. Geographical coding includes location of base or hospital.

DATA FORM: Logical Record

REFERENCE: Samuel A. Stouffer and other, *Studies in Social Psychology in World War II.* 4 Volumes, Published under the auspices of the Social Science Research Council (1949).

DATA STATUS: Available

CONTACT: Machine-Readable Archives Division, National Archives and Records Service.

1976 SURVEY OF INCOME AND EDUCATION (file Number: 2-235-78-2) Bureau of the Census for the Department of Health, Education and Welfare.

A sample of over 150,000 households statistically valid to the state level (all 50 states) and to SMSAs of over 250,000 population is the data base. Variables contained in the study include current labor force status, work experience, money income for 1975, age, sex, marital status, education, ethnicity, language spoken, migration history, disabilities, health insurance, mortgage and rent payments, and participation in food stamp and dependent child payment programs. State and city is also coded.

DATA FORM: Heirarchial, variable length record.

DATA STATUS: Available

CONTACT: Machine-Readable Archives Division, National Archives and Records Service.

SURVEY OF POPULATION (File Number: 3-220-75-122) Opinion Research Corporation for National Commission on Population Growth and the American Future.

The data is a nation-wide sample survey of 1,708 adults conducted in May-June, 1971. Variables incude level of political participation, attitudes toward the performance of federal, state and local government, attitudes toward population growth, knowledge of U.S. and world population levels, and attitudes toward immigration restriction, birth control, abortion, sterilization and sex education. Background variables include age, sex, race, marital status, number of children, education, religion, ethnicity, income, political party and desired number of children.

DATA FORM: Logical Record

DATA STATUS: Available

CONTACT: Machine-Readable Archives Division, National Archives and Records Service.

SOCIAL INDICATORS OF EQUALITY FOR MINORITIES AND WOMEN (File Number: C-453-79-1) United States Commission on Civil Rights.

Included are samples of 56,265 individuals from the state-20 %-public-use sample of the 1960 census, 153,715 individuals from the state-5 %-public-use sample of the 1970 census, 77,702 individuals from the state-15 %-public-use sample of the 1970 census, and 110,545 individuals from the public-use sample of the 1976 survey of income and education. Minorities are sampled at a higher rate than majority males. Information on family, residence, cost of housing, sources of income, expenses, education, occupational history and geographic mobility is coded. State of birth and state and place of residence at the time of the surveys and five years earlier for the decennial censuses are included. Size of area of residence is also a variable.

DATA FORM: Logical Record

REFERENCE: United States Commission on Civil Rights. *Social Indicators of Equality for Minorities and Women* (Washington, D.C., 1978).

DATA STATUS: Available

CONTACT: Machine-Readable Archives Division, National Archives and Records Service.

STATE AND LOCAL GOVERNMENT INFORMATION SURVEYS: 1973-1974 (File Number:3-403-76-5) United States Equal Employment Opportunity Commission.

The population is all local and state governments subject to the Equal Employment Opportunity Act of 1972 required to file reports. Reports are filed by functional activity. Variables include the number of employees in each functional activity by salary, sex and minority group. The address of the government reporting unit is included. There are 36,000 to 37,000 records for each year.

DATA FORM: Logical Record

DATA STATUS: Available

CONTACT: Machine-Readable Archives Division, National Archives and Record Service.

ELEMENTARY-SECONDARY STAFF INFORMATION SURVEYS, 1973-1974 (File Number: 3-403-76-6) United States Equal Employment Opportunity Commission.

The population is all public elementary and secondary school districts (6,600 for 1973, 7,600 for 1974) and all public elementary and secondary schools (69,000 for each year) subject to the Equal Employment Opportunity Act of 1972. The unit of analysis is the individual school district report or the individual school. There is one record each year for each report. Variables include the number of employees in each job classification by sex and minori - ty group. The SMSA and the address of the school district or the address of the school is included.

DATA FORM: Logical Record
DATA STATUS: Available
CONTACT: Machine-Readable Archives Division National Archives and Records Service.

SCHOOL TO COLLEGE: OPPORTUNITIES FOR POST HIGH SCHOOL EDUCATION: 1966-1970 (File Number: 3-419-79-2) Center For Research and Development in Higher Education and The University of California at Berkeley for the United States National Institute of Education.

The universe is a sample representing one cohort of students followed up over a five year period in California, Illinois, Massachusetts and North Carolina. Information on the respondent's sex, age, home state, academic ability, family and home milieu and values, perceptions of school, college and parental expectations, influences toward college, possible college majors, college activities and experiences, and attitudes about others, themselves, college and various social issues are present.

DATA FORM: Logical Record
DATA STATUS: Available
CONTACT: Machine-Readable Archives Division, National Archives and Records Service.

A COMPARATIVE STUDY OF PROPRIETARY AND NON-PROPRIETARY VOCATIONAL TRAINING PROGRAMS (File Number: 3-419-79-3).

The Data are a sample of people enrolled in one of four selected occupational programs: office, health, computer and technical fields in 46 vocational schools in the metropolitan areas of Atlanta, Chicago, Illinois, Rochester, New York, and San Francisco in the years 1969, 1970 or 1971. There are 5,963 cases. Variables coded include personal, educational and career information on the sampled alumni. Further education, age, race and sex are also included.

DATA FORM: Logical Record

REFERENCE: Steven M. Jung, and others, *Final Report: A Comparative Study Of Proprietary and Non-Proprietary Vocational Training Programs.* Volumes I and II. (Palo Alto, California: American Institutes For Research, 1972).

DATA STATUS: Available

CONTACT: Machine-Readable Archives Division, National Archives and Records Service.

NATIONAL LONGITUDINAL SURVEY, Young Women Center for Human Resources Research, Ohio State University, for The United States Employment Training Administration.

The data are a sample conducted by the Bureau of the Census of 5,159 civilian non-institutional women aged 14 through 24. The women were originally interviewed in 1968 and have been re-interviewed every two years for a period of ten years. Variables include race, sex, age, family size, marital status, income, employment, education, mobility, potential or actual jobs, and high school and college characteristics. A population-size indicator distinguishes rural areas and seven sizes of urban areas.

DATA FORM: Logical Record

DATA STATUS: Available

CONTACT: Machine-Readable Archives Division, National Archives and Records Service.

BOOK REVIEWS

THE ACHIEVEMENT OF MARGARET FULLER. By Margaret Vanderhaar Allen. *University Park and London: The Pennsylvania State University Press, 1979. Pp. xiii, 212. Index. Bibliography.*

THE MAKING OF A FEMINIST. EARLY JOURNALS AND LETTERS OF M. CAREY THOMAS. Edited by Marjorie Houspian Dobkin. *Kent State: The Kent State University Press, 1979. Pp. xvi, 314. Foreword by Millicent Carey McIntosh. Appendix. $15.00, cloth.*

Margaret Fuller's motto, "Give me truth, cheat me with no illusion," might well be a standard by which to measure recent contributions to women's history. Women historians of this generation, like the more overtly hagiographical biographers of the nineteenth and early twentieth centuries, face the dilemma illustrated most poignantly by Mary R. Beard's *Woman as a Force in History*: to emphasize the disabilities under which women have suffered or to stress the achievements they have contrived to patch together like quilts, which are now recognized as artistic creations.

Two new volumes indicate this dilemma; at the same time they probe new questions that may lead us to greater truth and less absorption in the quest for heroine-worship. A comparison of Margaret Vanderhaar Allen's intellectual biography of Margaret Fuller, concerned primarily "with Fuller's ideas and where they led her," (p. xii), and Marjorie Houspian Dobkin's well-edited selection of M. Carey Thomas' youthful journals and letters raises more significant issues than either volume analyzes directly. Dobkin's brief introductions to Thomas's life and to the chronologically-organized sections at least some of these more effectively than does Allen's work, albeit Allen begins with a provocative premise: that all of Fuller's biographers have cared more about her life than about her work. as part of the generation that has recognized the limited usefulness of models in seeking to transform economic, social and political institutions that limit the development of women, I think that the tangential issues raised by these works are more interesting than the deepened appreciation they elicit for their subjects.

The first of these issues is the influence of social class origins on a woman's aspirations and opportunities: on the initial confidence, courage and tangible resources with which she confronts the world's barriers. The class standings of Fuller and Thomas are dissimilar enough to remind one that the terrain labelled "white, middle-class elite" has peaks and valleys. While Fuller's family was that of a solidly professional and respectable New England lawyer, it cannot compare to that of Thomas's wealthy, socially prominent Baltimore Quaker family, a difference most clearly evident in Fuller's need to give up writing for employment as a schoolteacher at her father's untimely death and Thomas's need to ask her father not to ridicule her application for the presidency of Bryn Mawr, to ensure that his trustee friends take her seriously. The most fascinating tidbit of Dobkin's introduction, in fact, is that Thomas's first cousins were the first Mrs. Bertrand Russell and Mary Berenson, the wife of the noted art connoisseur, Bernard Berenson. both cousins were daughters of Thomas's rebellious Aunt Hannah Whitall Smith, who fled stuffy American Quakerism to live in London and who became Thomas's most ardent and calculating supporter in her effort to become the first president of Bryn Mawr (advising her to accept the Deanship and to become the first president after the male trustees had learned to accept her as an administrator).

This is not to say that being the daughter of a powerful family is an undivided path to achievement, as the difficulties attending Thomas's graduate study in Europe illustrate. While Fuller gave up her early-desired European trip because of the need to supplement her father's meagre legacy to his large family, Thomas *almost* gave up hers to assuage her family's fears that a respectable young women could not travel and study in Europe without tarnishing her reputation and disappointing her family's hopes. And while one senses that Fuller was driven to achieve out of financial necessity (not a mean force, as attested by Sam Johnson, Mark Twain and George Eliot), Thomas had to overcome the constraints of wealth and social connections that guarded as many doors as they opened to her.

Access to systematic education and encouragement for serious intellectual work likewise differed for the two not only because of growing acceptance of women in universities, but also, I suspect, because of their family backgrounds. No college existed in America for women when Margaret Fuller was in her teens, and she was tutored by her classically-educated father and her male peers who could attend Harvard. From them she learned the Classics and the disciplined use of language, and she was implicitly authorized by her father to become a serious thinker, which Allen argues she became. Thomas, coming of age in the 1870s, had many schools, both female and coeducational, to select from and chose Cornell University, partially, one suspects, because its president (Andrew White) was a member of her father's social class, and partially, Thomas's journal attests, because a co-ed degree represented "more than a Vassar one," (p. 116). both women felt that only men could challenge and guide them to intellectual merit; women, and in Thomas's case her mother and aunt Hannah, provided essential support but not the stimulation of male talent and assurance. (Allen, in fact, titles two of her chapters after influential men, "Emerson" and "Goethe.")

Both Fuller and Thomas, however, saw themselves as vanguards in the struggle to liberate women: Fuller from the dominance of male intellect and ideas; Thomas from the dominance of male academic institutions. Once again the difference bespeaks not only the increasing complexity of American institutions, but also notions and strategies of gaining power for women. For Fuller the problem was to free her own soul for creation and independent decisions; for Thomas, it was freeing women from limited knowledge and economic dependence on husbands and fathers, a goal she set for herself at the precocious age of fourteen. Fuller made her own life a model of risking and offering and persisting in the eccentricity of female decisiveness. Thomas made her college a center of advance scholarship and guarded its resources for women. One has the sense that Fuller dared more and that Thomas built more solidly (one passion, according to the introduction, being the construction of elegantly substantial buildings at Bryn Mawr).

A final issue raised by these women's lives and stimulated by Dobkin's discussion of Thomas's boarding school "smashes," is the connection between sexual adventurousness and intellectual creativity. In asserting that historians have confused the loving relationships of women's homosocial world with lesbian sexual practices, Dobkin says that Thomas was too conventional to have sexual relations with women and too aware of the consuming obligations of marriage to accept a man's advances, at least after she had committed herself to a career in women's education. While I agree with Dobkin's conclusion, Thomas's writings reveal a further reason: her fastidiousness about sensual contacts of all kinds. Thomas did not like "the flesh," and always felt that frivolous social contacts drained the energies essential for work.

Fuller not only sought sensual experience, terrifying her complacently married friend Emerson, but ultimately achieved a fusion of sexuality, political activism and writing in her devotion to the cause of Italian liberty and to Giovanni d'Ossoli, the patriot father of her son. Whether Fuller's manuscript on the history of the Roman republic would have justified her search cannot be known because it disappeared with her and her new Italian family in the shipwreck that cut off her life at forty. What we do know is that Thomas's much longer career produced only one notable manuscript, her summa cum laude thesis from Zurich. As Dobkin notes, despite her vow to write her autobiography, "She had not the patience to write for long," (p. 21).

Undoubtedly the creation of a great center of female learning is as important as the creation of a great book, but it is, perhaps, less imaginative and, finally, in its emulation, less threatening to the great centers of male learning and to other institutions of male authority and power. Fuller and Thomas represent two strategies for feminist action: pursuing truth for oneself no matter how eccentric the course and besting men's accomplishments no matter how confining the rules. The choice of strategies is still difficult, and Fuller and Thomas remind us of the immense value and hardship of pursuing either course. More importantly, I think, their lives challenge contemporary feminist scholars to think more carefully about how class origins, modes of legitimation, and psychosexual development hinder and help women in their pursuit of the milennium when, as Thomas said, we can realize that "liberty and money, independence and 'life work' are as much to a woman" as to a man, (p. 224).

Phyllis Marnick Palmer
The George Washington University

WOMEN, LAW, AND THE GENESIS TRADITIONS. By Calum M. Carmichael. *Edinburgh, Scotland: Edinburh University Press, 1979. Pp. 111.*

THE RIGHTS REVOLUTION. *Washington, D.C.: Congressional Quarterly, 1978. Pp. 217.*

Women, Law, and the Genesis Traditions is an examination by a professor of comparative literature of the laws in the Bible's book of Deuteronomy which concern women. The thesis is that these laws arose not to resolve particular problems commonly occurring at the time the laws were written, but rather in response to Israelite literary traditions from years before. These traditions were reported primarily in the book of Genesis. Thus, literary traditions, instead of customs, oracles or assemblies, served as the source of these laws.

Of interest is Professor Carmichael's assertion that the nature of these laws reflects a pair of goals held by the lawgiver who spoke through Moses. One of these goals was an attempt to minimize humiliation of women. The stories in Genesis often ended with the humiliation of women. Professor Carmichael observes that "time and again the lawgiver has taken stock of such occurrences" and "has not liked what he has seen." (p. 3). So the lawgiver issued laws which sought to uphold the honor of women. Nevertheless, this concern for the status of women was not a more general concern for the liberation from established roles. To the modern mind, the laws still seem repressive. The other of the goals was an attempt to provide an ideal model of behavior for the evolving Israelite nation. The stories in Genesis were updated to apply to the Israelite people, and the laws which arose in response to them were designed to expand national consciousness. If followed, these laws would show a contrast between Israelite and foreign behavior. The connection between this pair of goals is not apparent. Professor Carmichael, however, makes the connection clear by noting that the stories' incidents involving women, and the humiliation of them, "invariably" (p. 7) were due to foreign peoples' behavior. Therefore, the issuance of laws providing higher standards of sexual morality was an effort both to uphold the honor of women and to expand national consciousness. This conclusion does explain laws that previously seemed inexplicable—for example, the prohibition against plowing with an ox and an ass together. To support his argument Professor Carmichael analyzes stories in which women play a prominent role. These include the stories of Sarah, Rachel, Leah, Dinah, Bilhah, the daughters of Lot, Tamar and Ruth.

This book is not for the general reader. It takes up where a previous book by the author, *The Laws of Deuteronomy*, leaves off, and it presupposes considerable knowledge of the Old Testament. Nevertheless, a reader interested in the role of women in the Old Testament should find the book very helpful.

The Rights Revolution is a compendium of research reports on a variety of contemporary rights controversies. This compendium begins with an overview essay on the rights revolution and continues with reports on the equal rights amendment, Indian rights, access to legal services, media reform, political prisoners, right to death, reverse discrimination, anti-smoking campaign and prison policy.

These reports were published by *Congressional Quarterly* and sent to subscribers, such as journalists, to keep them up-to-date on developing issues and trends. Initially these reports were published between 1976 and 1978. As might be expected, they are quite timely. Though they do provide useful background information, the reports focus primarily on current aspects of the controversies. This is their advantage as well as their disadvantage. Their timeliness makes them very interesting. Consequently, the book would be appropriate as a supplementary text in an American politics course. On the other hand, their timeliness makes them likely to become dated more quickly than other writing on the same topics. (The editors already have had to insert notes explaining the Supreme Court's *Bakke* ruling.) But, for now, the book is well worth reading.

John Gruhl
The University of Nebraska at Lincoln

SEXISM AND THE LAW. A STUDY OF MALE BELIEFS AND LEGAL BIAS IN BRITAIN AND THE UNITED STATES. by Albie Sachs and Joan Hoff Wilson. *New York: The Free Press, 1978. pp. viii + 257. Bibliography. Index. $13.95.*

This book chronicles important aspects of the law's treatment of women in nineteenth and twentieth century Great Britain and the United States. With regard to Britain, focus is on attempts of women to invade what many saw as the male spheres of medicine and law and to enter public life through voting and holding office. In the "persons cases" which were brought to legitimate or challenge feminists' actions, the British judiciary consistently held that women were not "persons" in the same legal sense as were men and could therefore be denied the rights and privileges of full citizenship.

Similar issues arose in the United States in the nineteenth and twentieth centuries and, while legal forms differed, the outcome was the same as in Britain: women were not to be considered "persons" for the same intents and purposes as men. The women's movement of the nineteenth century aimed at reversing the trend of judicial decisions which permitted classification of the basis of sex and thus effectively denied women equality before the law. The efforts of activists such as Susan B. Anthony and Myra Colby Bradwell are fully discussed, as are the cases which arose as a result of feminist challenges to the established order.

The authors find a continuation of policies and ideologies that guarantee the legal subordination of women to men in the twentieth century. Moreover, the cause of that subordination—sexism—continues to flourish. While recent efforts at reform have been partly successful in both Britain and the United States, first-class citizenship still eludes women. Further remedies, such as the American equal rights amendment, are therefore necessary if women are to escape the legal disabilities under which they have lived for centuries.

The authors also discuss the treatment of women in contemporary legal professions. The point is made that women are seldom encouraged to seek a career in law and when they do, they are often subjected to rather cavalier treatment by peers and judges, in addition to being paid less than men. Sachs and Wilson argue that, at least with regard to the British legal profession, the advancement of women has been impeded for economic reasons, i.e., because the men who dominate that profession fear female competition. The book also contains a postscript on the Allan Bakke case, as appendix which lists important decisions and legislation in the nineteenth and twentieth centuries, and an appendix which provides statistics regarding the employment of women in the British and American legal professions.

This book has several strengths, of which the greatest is discussion of cases concerning women's rights within social and political contexts. Especially admirable are those sections dealing with American law and judicial interpretations of the fifth, fourteenth, and fifteenth amendments in the nineteenth and twentieth centuries.

The book is not, however, without flaws. Thus a reader may wonder at the claim, mentioned throughout and explicitly stated in the conclusion, that the authors have disposed "of at least two pieces of conventional wisdom," the first being "that legal systems evolve according to inherent principles of logic and procedure," and the second being "that historically the legal profession has acted as the guardian of the individual as against the public power." Yet surely these claims are men of straw, for few legal historians worthy of the name, and no lawyers except the most unsophisticated, would dare to argue either point. Admittedly the authors early on limit the idea of "judicial neutrality" to British jurists. But this book presumably aims at a much wider audience for whom the notion that law is influenced by ideologies and social, political and economic institutions will likely be commonplace.

A second criticism concerns the rather uneven quality of the sections on British and American law. Generally speaking, the portions dealing with the United States appear better researched and certainly better documented. Curiously, the footnotes to Chapter I, "Britain: Are Women 'Persons'?," do not list the page numbers of works cited. The same is occasionally true of the footnotes to the other chapters that deal with Britain.

Still, the book has much to offer. The sections concerning the United

States will serve as a helpful addition to such standard works in the field as Leo Kanowitz's *Women and The Law* and Aileen Kraditor's *Up From The Pedestal* and *Ideas of the Women's Suffrage Movement*, while the chapters dealing with Great Britain offer material not readily available elsewhere.

Janelle Greenberg
University of Pittsburgh

EQUAL RIGHTS AMENDMENT PROJECT. THE EQUAL RIGHTS AMENDMENT: A BIBLIOGRAPHIC STUDY. *Westport, Connecticut: Greenwood Press, 1976. pp. xxvii, 367. $19.95.*

It is sobering to reflect that when this book went to press in early 1976, full ratification of the equal rights amendment in the near future was confidently expected. Only four more states were needed to put a triumphant period to 55 years of struggle and controversy. The equal rights amendment project must therefore have considered it particularly timely to compile a list of sources for the still-unwritten history of the ERA. The resulting bibliography is perhaps more necessary now, as a cautionary reminder that the long time period covered by this book was simply the initial phase of a continuing effort.

The Equal Rights Amendment: a bibliographic study begins its coverage with the earliest published materials, including the first introduction of the proposed amendment in Congress (1923), and its advocacy by *Equal Rights*, the journal published by the National Woman's Party. Listings run forward from that point up to the early months of 1976. The bibliography includes a wide range of materials: federal and state government documents, books, dissertations, periodical articles and even ephemeral pamphlets and brochures. Some 5,800 references are listed in all (including some duplication in the cases of items which appeared in more than one source). Coverage is heavily weighted toward periodical and newspaper articles, which account for more than half the citations. The smallest (and consequently weakest) section is a chapter that references books, articles and discussions appearing as part of books, and dissertations: only 59 items are listed here.

Many of the citations for pamphlets and other small (often obscure) publications were derived from the *Herstory* and *Women and the Law* microfilm collections compiled by the Women's History Research Center in Berkeley. Although these two collections present certain difficulties to the researcher (difficulties which are duly noted in the introduction), indexing their ERA-related contents was especially helpful for several reasons. Good guides to the WHRC microfilms were not previously available, making their use difficult. The filmed collections are owned by numerous libraries, so that access is comparatively easy. Finally, they include some materials which are not commonly (or not at all) found in other locations

Perhaps the least necessary part of the book may be a large section (over 1,600 references) covering articles, letters and editorials in newspapers. These references include papers which are already fully indexed, such as the *Chicago Tribune* and *Washington Post*. There are also items from *Editorials on File*, and additional citations from the *Herstory* and *Women and the Law* microfilms. Since most of these listings can be found in other sources (or even, as with the *New York Times*, are available through automated searches), the need to duplicate them here might be questioned. Perhaps, however, having so many references to the equal rights amendment grouped conveniently in one place is sufficient justification in itself.

The chapter on material published in periodicals contains four sections in addition to newspapers. *Equal Rights*, published by the National Woman's Party between 1923 and 1954, has a section of its own. Law reviews are grouped together. A large, herterogeneous section combines "academic journals, popular magazines, and special interest newspapers." (These range from feminist periodicals like *Off Our Backs* and *Majority Report* to *Newsweek, Congressional Quarterly Weekly Report, Good Housekeeping* and *Senior Scholastic*. Comparatively few "academic" journals are included.) The remaining section, called "Newsletters," is potentially one of the most useful in the bibliography, since most of the items cited are not indexed elsewhere. This section can be used to retrieve listings from local NOW chapter journals (primarily), and from the *John Birch Society Bulletin* and the *Phyllis Schlafly Report*. Many of the citations in this section also were derived from the *Herstory* and *Women and the Law* microfilm collections.

The Equal Rights Amendment: a bibliographic study has been carefully organized. Each section is preceded by an explanatory note defining its scope; helpful comments are frequent. The unsigned introductory essay provides an excellent concise history of the proposed equal rights amendment and controversies surrounding it up to 1976, plus a good description of the plan and content of the book itself. There are two useful indexes appended, one of authors and the other of organizations. The latter gives addresses, where known. This could be of considerable help to researchers desirous of contacting particular groups, although an editorial note wisely cautions that "addresses are impossible to provide with complete accuracy due to both their somewhat rapid birth and demise and their peripatetic nature", (p. 348). An interesting preface describes the Equal Rights Amendment Project itself: initially established with Rockefeller Foundation money through the California Commission on the Status of Women, its activities between 1974 and publication of this book were intended to "assist in the process of change" which was expected to result from passage of the ERA, (p. vii). At the very least, it can be said that the Project contributed in significant ways to the compilation and distribution of ERA-related information.

In approaching this bibliography, one must be aware of its limitations. The most serious of these, from the research standpoint, is that it includes only published materials. The book's usefulness could have been considerably enhanced by the addition of information about archival records of the National Women's Party and other groups and about extant collections of correspondence, diaries or other unpublished writings by major figures involved in the history of the ERA. Regrettably, it is necessary to seek this information elsewhere. Another point which might be made is that the bibliography could have been better constructed to suit its most likely potential users. Clearly, the primary market for it is to be found in libraries. Few if any libraries would be likely to have all the items cited readily available in their own collections, meaning that access to many materials needed by researchers would involve the use of interlibrary loan channels. Retrieval of information needed for ILL purposes could have been facilitated by including references, where appropriate, to National Union Catalog listings, Library of Congress card numbers, OCLC record numbers, and/or ISBN/ISSN numbers.

This book is not the definitive bibliography of the equal rights amendment. However, it can provide good starting points for research into ERA history, and it is particularly valuable for information about obscure and ephemeral materials.

Edith M. Bjorklund
University of Wisconsin-Milwaukee

BIGOTRY!: ETHNIC, MACHINE, AND SEXUAL POLITICS IN A SENATORIAL ELECTION. By Maria J. Falco. *Westport, Conn.: Greenwood Press, 1980, Pp. xvi & 200. Bibliography. Index. $18.95.*

Ms. Falco has written a clear and lively account of the 1964 Senatorial race in Pennsylvania, capturing its drama and conflict. According to Ms. Falco, this election campaign illustrates three important phenomena in American politics: the awakening of ethnic political consciousness; the decline of city-based political machines; and the fact of political bias against women. Her account certainly does portray the deteriorating power of Pennsylvania's state and city Democratic organizations. She also shows how bitter primary battles accelerate the party's decline and make victory in the general election nearly impossible. Further, she provides an excellent description of Pennsylvania's political climate and background.

The story mainly concerns the battle for the Democratic nomination for Senator between Genevieve Blatt, a long-time party official and office holder, and Micheal A. Musmanno, a colorful state Supreme Court Justice, who had the backing of the Philadelphia machine. By campaigning as a political reformer, Ms. Blatt was able to narrowly defeat her party-backed opponent in the primary. However, some of the campaign rhetoric of her supporter, Senator Joseph Clark, had created bad feeling among some of the Italian-American organizations in the state; and the closeness of the race had led to lengthy recounts and court fights concerning voting fraud. As a result, Ms. Blatt went into the general election facing many handicaps. She was unable to unseat Senator Hugh Scott despite the fact that President Johnson's landslide victory was pulling many Democratic candidates into office on his coattails.

Although Ms. Falco presents an interesting historical account of these events and includes valuable appendices and bibliography, one might question the focus of her analysis. Her major concern is to explain why Ms. Blatt lost the general election. Consequently, she concentrates on three factors in the election: the ethnic question and how Italians perceived an alleged slur; the possible retaliation of the Democratic party leaders against a reform candidate; and voter bias against a female candidate for national office. She concludes that these factors were important causes of the defeat; however, the evidence she presents is far from conclusive. Voting analysis showed that Italian voters did not give Scott any greater support than did other ethnic minorities who generally voted Democratic. The impact of machine opposition in a general election is not likely to be great. It certainly did not prevent her from winning the primary. According to opinion polls, the net effect of her sex would cost Ms. Blatt approximately 3% of the vote.

In view of all the facts presented by Ms. Falco, it is hardly surprising that Ms. Blatt lost. Under the circumstances, it is easy to imagine her losing without the presence of any of the three factors discussed. She was not declared the winner of the primary until August 19, and appeals continued until October 12. Her campaign was badly organized, and, in terms of time, money, staff and strategy, "woefully inadequate" (p. 112). She never developed a theme, and her shots at Scott tended to win him "more admiration than criticism" (p. 106). She based her strategy on one generally inaccurate poll. On the other hand, Senator Scott began campaigning thirteen months ahead of her with "competent, professional results" (p. 112). As Falco notes, his campaign manager was the "man best equipped for the job" (p. 112). Scott had better television advertising and "one of the most prominent and experienced pollsters in the state" (p. 113).

Ms. Blatt did not have any of the characteristics needed to overcome the normal advantages enjoyed by an incumbent. She was not a colorful, charismatic person, and there were no skeletons in Scott's closet. Her only asset was President Johnson's overwhelming landslide, and Ms. Falco points out that his coattails failed to carry all Democrats to power in other states as well. Further, Ms. Falco states that Pennsylvania has been a swing state since 1954 where the people are "almost eager to demonstrate their independence by splitting their tickets" (p. 18). Republicans and Democrats regularly share victories in state elections. Since Senator Scott was a relatively popular incumbent whose moderate policies were favorably viewed by the voters, the big surprise is that he won by only 70,000 votes. One would have expected him to coast to re-election by a comfortable margin.

Despite Ms. Falco's strained efforts to attribute Blatt's loss to bigotry charges and sexual bias, the book presents an interesting case study which dramatizes recent trends in American politics. This election was indicative of the rise in importance of ethnic politics and the decline of election control by party machines.

Janet Clark
New Mexico State University

WOMEN MAKING IT - PATTERNS AND PROFILES OF SUCCESS.
By Ruth Halcomb. *New York: Atheneum, 1979. Pp.335. Index. Notes.*
Sources. $13.95.

Are you a successful career woman or do you want to become one? What
is a successful professional woman? Are there special characteristics or activities which help women succeed? While this journalistic-style book probably will not answer all these questions to your satisfaction, it will help you
understand how you compare to others and provide you with fresh feminist
insights on success in your profession.

Ruth Halcomb's ideas on "Women Making It" come from interviews
with forty successful women, general reading in the area and her own experiences and common sense. This book is not careful scientific study based
on comparable interviews with women selected to meet predetermined
criteria for success. Nor does it criticize or synthesize a comprehensive body
of related research on career development of women or men. Due however,
to the author's broad perspective, the insights shared in this book are likely
to be more relevent to most career women than individual scientific studies
such as Hennig's and Jardim's *The Managerial Woman.*

The major themes of this book suggest that: 1) Successful women are
not isolates. Many are married, have children and active lives apart from
their jobs; 2) Successful women are somewhat different from successful men
and need not copy male patterns of success; 3) Many successful women make
special efforts to help other women and the women's movement. To the extent possible, Ruth Halcomb focuses on things women can change in their
lives, such as seizing opportunities for advancement or maintaining em-
pathetic relationships, rather than those characteristics they can't change,
such as the number of siblings they have.

Despite this effort, the author does not attempt to advise women on what
they should do to succeed in their careers. She merely relates what seems
important to some successful women. Many are influenced by encouraging
parents and role models. Some of her interviewees had clear initial visions
of their career goals. Others focused on what they wanted to do gradually.
Many of the women Ruth Halcomb interviewed seemed to achieve success
after some major challenge in their lives, such as a personal crisis. She indicated that most seemed to act genuinely and did not appear to be too
feminine or feminist. Some of the interviewees acknowledged help of mentors or from networks.

Many of the themes, such as the roles of mentors and networks and the
issue of women competing with or helping other women, could each be the

subject of their own fascinating books. Six of the chapters begin with detailed interviews with a woman in a particular career area, such as Eleanor Holmes Norton in public service and Carolyn See, a writer, and then generalize to provide information about women in these careers. An alternative future effort could compare different attributes of successful women in all these career areas. Such an analysis may help women choose career paths in the 1980s.

In summary, this book is easy, enjoyable reading and may provide readers with insights about themselves and their professional women colleagues. There is plenty of room to build on this optimistic work by clarifying vague concepts, such as the definition of a successful woman, and by presenting more comprehensive balanced views of how a side range of successful women made it. Future efforts, also may describe more valid and comprehensive images of successful career women by discussing how they coped with negative aspects of their lives, such as career setbacks, and frequent personal and family sacrifices. Future publications on successful women advance Ruth Halcomb's initial attempt to understand how women can be encouraged to identify and use strategies to make it on their own terms rather than deliberately choosing male success strategies.

Susan S. Klein
National Institute of Education,
Education Department

THE ECONOMICS OF SEX DIFFERENTIALS. By Cynthia B. Lloyd and Beth T. Niemi. *New York: Columbia University Press, 1979. P. xvi, 326. Index. Bibliography. Tables. Figures. $16.50.*

Economists typically enjoy developing rigorous, analytical models of decision processes from first principles. Often this penchant for formal theorizing produces research whose meaning is unclear to noneconomists. While Lloyd and Nieni do sometimes present microeconomic theory in formalistic textbook terms, they are generally successful at producing clear verbal explanations of how hypotheses are developed, how sophisticated statistical procedures can be used to test these hypotheses effectively, and how these tests produce results useful for policy analysis.

The study analyzes determinants of male-female differences in wages, earnings, labor force participation and unemployment. The approach is based on two conflicting theories of labor force behavior The first of these traditional neoclassical theory emphasizes the determination of wage and employment levels on the basis of strict assumptions about the nature of labor and product markets. When examining sex discrimination, this theory tends to place relatively great explanatory weight on male-female differences in labor supply. The segmented labor market theory, on the other hand, places relatively greater weight on differences in the factors determining demand (expecially costs of training and retaining a labor force) across occupations.

Chapters 1 and 2 analyze the extent to which difference in the economic status of men and women can be explained by differences in willingness to work. Lloyd and Niemi discuss four aspects of the labor supply decision: the probability that the individual is in the labor force, number of hours worked per week, number of weeks worked per year and the length of time that a person is likely to be continually at work without unemployment. Particular attention is devoted to studies which measure the impact on time spent doing housework by husbands and time spent with children as a result of decisions by wives to increase their hours of paid work.

In Chapter 3 the authors consider the effects of education and training. After a textbook treatment of human capital theory applied both to formal education and to informal on-the-job training, there is a short but interesting review of research on the impact of women's formal education on husband's incomes and children's achievements. The chapter ends with a discussion of the impact of differential training opportunities for women on differential occupational mobility.

In Chapters 4 and 5 the authors assess the impact of discrimination on earnings and employment. Factors affecting wage and employment levels can be viewed as falling into three categories: first, those only minimally related to discrimination, such as wage level difference due to city size or location; second, social traditions which, through the normal functioning of labor markets, result in lower salaries or labor force participation for women (such as training and experience, and differing marital roles); and third, discriminatory behavior which cannot be rationalized by objective, if "unfair," differences between the sexes. There is considerable discussion of the relationship of the costs of training a stable and technically able labor force to the wages employers are willing to pay, the value to employers of screening devices used to identify those workers most likely to reward the employer's training efforts, and the inaccuracy of using sex as a screening device. The authors carefully review a number of empirical studies which try to estimate how much of the wage or employment gap is justified by differences in productivity between the sexes, and how much is due to discrimination.

The authors turn in Chapter 6 to the way in which government affects economic discrimination against women. Topics analyzed include the impacts on female economic status of inequities in the progressive income tax system, social security, the welfare system and unemployment insurance. Other public programs analyzed include general macroeconomic policy, employment and training programs and minimum wage laws. The chapter concludes with a review of recent legal developments. The final chapter discusses the difficulty in making projections of women's future labor force activity and considers whether female employment and earning are likely to change in the next decade.

The Economics of Sex Differentials is a very well done book. The discussions of the research literature are interesting and extremely up-to-date; a large proportion of the research that is summarized was published in 1978 or 1979. The authors never overburden the reader with econometric detail, but do indicate when a particular procedure has been used inappropriately. Both noneconomists and economists will find the book extremely useful for learning in a hurry the current state of the art on research into women's economic status. In addition, it could very reasonably be used as the core textbook in courses focusing on women in the labor market.

Marsha Goldfarb
University of Maryland, Baltimore County

ABORTION IN AMERICA: THE ORIGINS AND EVOLUTION OF NATIONAL POLICY, 1800-1900. By James C. Mohr. *New York: Oxford University Press, 1979. Pp. x, 331. Index. Appendices. $4.95, paper.*

Abortion in America is an example of how scholarly historical research can serve to illuminate current social controversy. In this case, today's dilemma is over a woman's right to have legal access to abortion. Popular belief would have it that abortion has always been considered the taking of a life, particularly by church officials; that legislators have historically been firm in their goal to outlaw abortion; and that physicians have supported a woman's right to terminate pregnancy safely.

These myths are destroyed in Mohr's fascinating tracing of the legal status of abortion in the United States from 1800-1900. Described is the relative freedom of the 1800 American (or British) woman to seek abortion. This freedom was due to the absence of legislation covering abortion, as well as the average citizen's ignorance that pregnancy begins before fetal movement is felt.

The period before 1820 was exemplified by a lack of concern regarding abortion. For the next two decades, however, legislation in states and territories was passed, due to care for women's health (poisons and crude surgical equipment were used to abort) and through a growing fear by trained physicians of the popularity of medical practitioners who were "irregular" or non-certified physicians. This can be seen, in part, by the fact that these new anti-abortion laws were designed to punish the abortion administrator, rather than penalize the pregnant woman for having sought abortion. Indeed, Mohr skillfully pinpoints the evolution of abortion policy as being intertwined with the history of medical practice and status of physician.

It was those same physicians, eager to raise their status above that of the "irregular," who played a questionable role in nineteenth century public policy-making. Through their attempts to drive abortion-performing "irregulars" out of the medical marketplace, they succeeded in nearly outlawing legal abortion for American women by the end of the century. Mohr states that physicians were the "single most important factor in altering the legal policies toward abortion in the country" (p. 157).

There were, other variables which contributed to the shift in abortion law. The commercialization of abortion, shown by advertisements placed by abortionists in the daily newspapers, raised the visibility of the incidence of abortion in America. There was a corresponding upsurge in the number of abortions performed (as well as in the practice of contraception), and a decline of the birth rate. As the American public became aware of these conditions, the typical women who sought abortion changed.

In the early nineteenth century, the average abortion seeker was an unmarried young woman who sought to obliterate her condition. By the middle of the nineteenth century, however, the typical abortion patient was a married woman who used abortion as another form of birth control. This woman was married, native-born, middle or upper-class and Protestant. There was a fear that Protestants' low birth rates would leave immigrants to reproduce the future generations of Americans.

As in abortion conflicts today, certain people also feared the consequences of allowing women to determine their own reproductive future. Women's higher status, its appropriateness within the needs of the family and its conflict with men's desire for control contributed toward increasingly restrictive policies in regard to abortion in many states and territories.

Physicians influenced the discussion of abortion whenever they could and hoped to draw church officials into the conflict. Although they failed at this, physicians were aided by the 1873 Federal anti-obscenity law, enforced by special agent Anthony Comstock. (Comstock's role in suppressing birth control information is aptly discussed in David M. Kennedy's *Birth Control In America*.) Through the banning of abortion advertisement, abortionists were either prosecuted or driven underground. By 1880, more than 40 anti-abortion statutes in states and territories were in place, and women themselves were arrested for having sought or undergone abortions. Abortions were further restricted by defining pregnancy from conception, rather than from the beginning of fetal movement. Unbelievably, these laws remained in effect for nearly 100 years, until *Roe vs. Wade*.

Since there was no real federal role in abortion until the Comstock Act in 1873, Mohr's book is somewhat misnamed. Prior to that, and until the Supreme Court decision of 1973, abortion regulation was a state or territorial matter. Indeed, Mohr shows how this social issue has become an example of the lessening strength of state rights, referred to as federal ''intrusion'' by the Republican party platform in 1976. Mohr's volume can be used as the best example of how painstaking historical research can help students of public policy understand the variations and nuances of policy in the making. It hardly needs to be added that students of medical history, birth control in America or women's rights would be interested in this work; or, for that matter, anyone seeking a fascinating look into our past.

Janice Pottker
U.S. Department of Education

WE WILL SMASH THIS PRISON! INDIAN WOMEN IN STRUGGLE.
By Gail Omvedt. *London: Zed Press, 1980. Pp. 189. Appendices. Glossary.*
Bibliographical Notes. Map. $6.95, Paper. $17.95, Cloth.

The field of women and politics has primarily focused on industrialized
nations. Recent work on women and development has begun to correct the
imbalance, but few studies have treated non-elite women as political subjects; instead they are seen solely as victims. Thus Gail Omvedt's *We Will
Smash This Prison! Indian Women in Struggle* is a valuable resource, because
it depicts the process of women mobilizing against oppression in one third-
world nation. Omvedt is an American scholar and activist who has spent
ten years studying and participating in movements for social change among
the poor in Maharashtra, a state in Western India. This book is her account
of ten months spent in Maharashtra in 1975.

The book is "written to bring to others something of a reality of Indian
women's aspirations and struggles as [Omvedt] experienced them at the
time" (p. 155). Although she writes from a Marxist perspective, the book
is remarkably jargon-free. Revolutionary songs of activists begin the chapters
which center around portraits of women, ranging from an agricultural laborer
untouched by current organizing efforts, to women intermittently affected,
women who form the base of militant organizations, leaders of left parties
and feminist activists. Omvedt traces the genesis of a Women's Liberation
Conference held on October 1975. It takes place despite the Emergency im-
posed by Prime Minister Indira Gandhi in June 1975, as women's issues are
considered social not political. Nevertheless, the Emergency affects the conference; the left is divided, many of the left's activities are abandoned, and
leaders are underground or imprisoned.

Throughout the book women articulate what oppression means to them,
and Omvedt adds background material. Patriarchal cultural traditions (e.g.,
dowry) affect all but the *dalit* (untouchable) and tribal women, and they suffer
rape by Hindu landlords. Indian women face the double burden of economic
discrimination and shrinking employment opportunities. But the women portrayed by Omvedt do not passively accept their growing victimization. The
struggles they wage vary in organizational focus, method and outcome. The
left parties use top-down methods to organize working class agitations in
urban and rural areas. There is a broad women's front, the Anti-Price Rise
Committee. Twenty thousand women march against inflation wielding roll-
ing pins, but the top-down methods of the left parties result in the Committee's demise during the Emergency. A tribal organization with women at
the forefront that wins back land from Hindu farmers exemplifies more of

a grass roots effort. A middle class feminist group, the Progressive Organization of Women, wary of the traditional left, experiences some success organizing women students around cultural issues but is crushed by the Emergency because of its ties to the revolutionary left.

In an afterword Omvedt attempts to assess the significance of the mobilizing efforts she has described. While there has been an increase in consciousness, little long-lasting organizational development has occurred among the masses. Omvedt characterizes the left parties with their top-down organizational methods as bankrupt and the middle class feminists as unable to organize the masses. For a women's movement to develop in India, she believes grass roots women's organizations must be formed in coalition with a broader urban or rural working class movement. She remains cautiously optimistic that this can occur.

The book's major strength lies in its vivid descriptions of the Indian women activists and their social context. Based on my knowledge of the personalities described, I would judge the portraits to be accurate. More participant observer work of this kind is needed to document the rich variety of women's participation in social movements worldwide. A weakness lies in the book's exclusive focus on mobilization and thus neglect of policy making. While this reflects Omvedt's lack of faith in electoral politics, two of the left activists she interviews have had substantial experience as legislators at the municipal, state and national levels. Questions concerning the conditions under which feminist policy makers can play effective roles in women's liberation, which policy reforms are worth fighting for and how activists can keep feminist legislators honest are important for scholars and activists to consider in the Indian case and in comparative analysis.

Jana Everett
University of Colorado at Denver

BENGALI WOMEN. By Manisha Roy. *Chicago: The University of Chicago Press, 1975. Pp. xvii + 205. Appendix. Index. Illustrations. References. $4.95, paper.*

In this anthropological/psychological study of *Bengali Women*, Manisha Roy (herself of such origin) takes us through the life cycle of a typical upper class Hindu woman within the modern Bengali joint family, depicting the "frustrations and compensations" that such a woman experiences in her many social roles. Only one who knows the author personally could tell whether she intended this study as an indictment of the joint family system, for she never offers any explicit judgment about its merits or its long-term impact on the psyche and on social relations. Once only does she venture to make a judgement when in a historical context, she refers to the "degradation" of women in the latter part of the eighteenth century, as the result of the institution of strict endogamy introduced by orthodox Brahams, which led to hypergamy and *sati* (the practice of self-immolation by a widow on the funeral pyre of her husband). Thereafter, she gives us a dispassionate account of the frustrations (a mild term in light of what unfolds) that begin for the woman at around age 20 when she goes to her husband's home to begin her life-long career as wife and mother. Yet, one must be grateful to tha author because the moving picture she projects, starting particularly with the third chapter on marriage and going through the "Later Years and Old Age" is so compelling in documenting the woman's emotional and intellectual straitjacket, that it must stir the conscience of even the most traditional of men (especially Bengalis, if they are inclined to read this), and certainly it must awaken the consciousness of more traditional women.

Whether Roy intended it so, the study emerges as just such as indictment. It is difficult to read this sensitive, subtle account without a sense of horror and anger at a system which so relentlessly crushes the woman's identity, ignores her needs and distorts her aspirations in order to preserve a social system—the Bengali version of the joint family—designed by men and for men, in a man's world. The tragic irony is that both men and women are socially and psychologically stunted by such a system. Their emotional life is painfully fragmented. A man cannot seek friendship, companionship, romance, sexual pleasure and respect from his wife, but rather must find these (and partially at best) in men and women outside and within the joint family, But our sympathies are more strongly drawn to the woman who has few if any of the many outlets enjoyed by the man.

If one took all the stereotypes of woman familiar to us, added all the inequities accompanying the woman's condition in her darkest periods, included the phenomenon of the acceptance of these by the woman herself in a spirit of sacrifice and resignation, with the resulting loss of identity and self-esteem, and tried to construct the most grotesque model of the conditions under which a woman could exist, one might well come up with the reality that emerges in the society Roy describes. We find here the starkest stereotype of the woman as whore or goddess, mistress or mother; the definition of woman wholly in terms of the men in her life; the desirability of motherhood as the "ultimate achievement" of woman; the ideal of total sacrifice of personal needs and aspirations for the sake of husband and sons; the wife as wholly the ornament of man; the perception of sex as dirty and instigated by woman.

The most cruel injury inflicted on the Bengali woman, however, results from her socialization during childhood and adolescence, a process which builds up romantic fantasies and expectations about married life (through the media education and the literature—religious and secular—to which she is exposed), only to have these expectations mercilessly and systematically dashed. Sex is the one personal pleasure and need that woman can and does look forward to—from adolescence onward. But though not denied her in marriage, it is mechanical and totally shorn of the romance and excitement which she had learned to associate with the husband of her dreams—her own personal "deity" (as he is symbolized in the wedding ceremony).

Sexual union with the wife has no purpose other than to have a son. And for the woman, the role of mother is the only one that assures her respect, emotional satisfaction and security. As the "ultimate achievement," it is understandably coveted by the woman, for she soon discovers as a new wife that the most lasting and satisfying relationship within the joint family is that between mother and son. Outside of that, there is no acceptable, respectable way in which a woman can fulfill herself in society.

While Roy maintains that the system provides compensations for the frustrations it generates for women, these compensations seem inadequate recompense for what is denied: the love, companionship and respect of her husband; her sense of identity; self-actualization; and her freedom to make important personal choices throughout her life. What are the compensations? There is, firstly, a peculiar kind of romantic relationship that develops between the new wife and her *debar* (the younger, unmarried brother-in-law) which satisfies in part her romantic fantasies ("peculiar" because, suprisingly, it is sanctioned in the joint family system, as long as it does not develop into an overt sexual affair). With the birth of the first child, she begins to enjoy some status in the family, which is further enhanced if the baby is male. She also begins to enjoy a more relaxed and affectionate relationship with her husband who feels more "comfortable" with her, now that the purpose of their sexual union has been visibly fulfilled. When the children grow up, she may enjoy wielding authority in the household (if she has the type of personality which finds this appealing and if other conditions allow). She may command more respect and feel wanted—indeed indispensable. At the same time (or as an alternative), she can develop a relationship with a *guru* (usually a handsome and somewhat younger man) through whom she can aspire to realize God. This, too, has romantic overtones (again, without sex). But the guru is someone to whom she can offer all the repressed and suppressed feelings of love for which there has been no outlet provided by her husband. In both of these cases, the forbidden fruit of sexual love is dangled before her, but kept just a millimeter beyond reach (though some—perhaps many more than this study suggests—do make that reach). These, then, are the "compensations," and most of them come rather late in life, if they come at all, and are always tentative.

In short, the picture of the woman that emerges is first, of a reproductive machine. She is the womb for man—literally and figuratively. Second, she is the ultimate "stroker" of the husband and the males among her in-laws and the elders (men and women) in her husband's family. While *sati* is no longer practiced, it nevertheless survives in a cultural/social form where the woman is, as it were, burned at the altar of the joint family and the male's needs.

The shortcomings of this book (which include some unnecessary jargon) are far outweighed by its merits. It makes a fine contribution to the comparative literature on the study of women.

Mary C. Carras
Rutgers University
Camden, New Jersey

MUSLIM WOMEN IN MOMBASA 1890-1975. By Margaret Strobel. *New Haven: Yale University Press, 1979. Pp.xii + 258. Index. Bibliography. Tables. $19.50.*

Margaret Strobel's *Muslim Women in Mombasa 1890-1975* is a fascinating study of the patterns of continuity and change within Muslim society, particularly among women, in the coastal region of Kenya. The context of the study is the impact of the forces of colonialism, Christianity and capitalism on the seacoast town of Mombasa. In 1890, Mombasa was a Muslim town where slavery was still practiced; today it is the major seaport for the entire East African region and a commercial and industrial center in its own right. In ethnic, as well as racial and cultural terms, Mombasa continues to be a city of great diversity. This growing heterogeneity, and the reaction to it of the Muslim community, form a central theme of the book.

Muslim Women in Mombasa is both very well-researched and very well written. Strobel is concerned to link her study with relevant literatures and debates in anthropology, womens' studies and Kenyan history. She displays a remarkable breadth of scholarly concern and knowledge that allows *Muslim Women* to speak to the concerns of all three literatures. Her footnotes contain a wealth of useful sources, comments and comparisons. Luckily, this documentation does not distract from the very interesting story that Strobe has to tell. She deserves a great deal of credit for being able to combine her various theoretical concerns and the highly complex nature of the topic into a very readable book.

Muslim Women is organized around the interaction of ethnicity, sex and class. The author is very careful to avoid giving primacy to any of the three factors. The study is particularly concerned with the impact of colonial incorporation on male-female relations and attitudes and the various institutional modes that Muslim women developed in response to the changing contexts in which they lived. Strobe refrains from any form of "villains and heroes" approach that sees the colonial impact as either a conspiracy of oppression or as a liberator from a sexually repressive Islam. In fact, perhaps the most interesting finding of the book is the manner in which the nature of female oppression and subordination is transformed under the impact of the various changes emanating from colonial incorporation. One of the highlights of the book is the chapter on the marginalization of women's work in Mombasa in the course of the twentieth century. Strobel argues that while colonialism has in several ways weakened the direct subordination of females to males in the Mombasa Muslim community, it has not created an independent material base upon which women could emerge as equals to men.

Flowing out of the context of sexual segregation in Muslim society, a women's sub-culture, expressed in both institutional and cultural forms, emerged in Mombasa. Strobel pays particular attention to the role of various forms of dance in this sub-culture. The chapter on "lelemama" dance associations is particularly provocative. Strobel argues that these dance associations are an expression of and forum for social stratafication among Muslim women, and looks at their changing make-up over time.

It is impossible in such a short review to give a full sense of the richness of *Muslim Women in Mombasa*. Professor Strobel has very creatively com-bined archival and oral sources to convey a living and dynamic feel for her subjects. In her work she links an awareness and concern with theory with the ability to tell an interesting story. Anthropologists, historians of Africa and women's studies scholars will all find this book important and interesting.

David F. Gordon
The University of Michigan

THE CURIOUS COURTSHIP OF WOMEN'S LIBERATION AND SOCIALISM. By Batya Weinbaum. *Boston, Mass.: South End Press, 1978. Pp. ix, 168. $4.00, paper.*

Batya Weinbaum's *Curious Courtship* is a forceful and provocative at-tempt to illuminate fruitful areas of investigation into the relation of feminism, socialism and psychoanalysis. In tying the history of the interac-tion between feminism and socialism as political movements in with theoretical differences in their analyses, Weinbaum provides a perspective from which Marx, Engels and contemporary socialist ideology on "the woman question" look distinctly phallocentric. As an alternative, she sug-gests a synthesis of the paradigms of sex, class and generational struggle into one set of "kin" categories. While certain of her insights remain valuable, her collapse of kin categorization into Freudian Fathers and "primal hoarding brothers" severely compromises her ability to clarify the dynamic processes of women's oppression.

Weinbaum's vagueness in crucial spots points to more fundamental prob-lems besetting her work: its own phallocentric definitions. For example, she argues that kinship catergories are the most basic, but seems unsure of their exact ontological status. She then takes the category of the Father from Freud as nonproblematic, when in fact there are good reasons to think that Freud's theory of the construction of sexuality is culture-bound and male-biased and contains dualistic and hierarchical assumptions about human nature and our relation to the rest of the natural world.

Weinbaum's debts to Levi-Strauss's and Gayle Rubin's readings of Freud cause her further trouble when she attempts to apply the oedipal rebellion myth to socialist revolutions. Structuralist analyses identify exchange relations, which Rubin argues impose a conventional "cultural organization"on procreation, as the essential element of kinship. However, to conceptualize exchange as the definitive feature of social interaction divorces the human, cultural processes from the natural, necessary ones, sets them at odds and obscures the chain of relations between the two. For relations of exchange to exist at one level, relations of production, which *presuppose* a sexual division of labor, must exist at another. The latter creates conditions of hostility among adult men. Thus, relations of exchange cannot *explain* the sexual division of labor.

The problems generated by exchange theories surface when Weinbaum tries to spell out the concept of male sexual jealousy in terms of women as socialist men's property. Her first interpretation of radical feminism, namely, "woman's control of woman's body," gets transformed into "the feminist notion of women as property". She then argues that this "feminist notion" can fruitfully be integrated with the Freudian tradition of women as property and the Marxist concept of abolishing private property in legalistic terminology. With this, she has slipped into a discourse at the level of exchange and not production, and has the wrong vocabulary for articulating the real processes of power.

Thus, before we conclude this proposed merger, we need to ask why one should think that such a heterosexual coupling needs to be "insured" in the first place. Would males and females be radically separate without a sexual division of labor which enjoins obligatory heterosexuality? Without one, men and women might instead look 'radically similar.'

The dualistic theory of human nature, that is, the belief that human beings are split into two warring parts—their minds and their sexual bodies—implicit in these approaches blocks questioning of this assumption. The male-directed revolt against the flesh and desire for transcendence form the mainstays of theories which treat needs-to-dominate as responses to an eternally hostile world.

Yet, as feminists and materialists, we need to critique our way out of dualistic conceptualizations, rather than "recombine" elements of male-defined theories. These exchange theories break down into more traditional, sexist views over the important issues of mind-body dualism, the relation between sex and gender, and their differentiation into hierarchical pairs. This should lead us to adopt another apprach, one which would not (i) read exchange relations back into pre-state and pre-historic societies, and (ii) view the sexual division of labor as an arbitrary, conventional way to insure reciprocity. Until we no longer conceptualize history as the struggle of MEN, we will repeat its oppressions within our theories and strategic activities.

Annette M. Bickel
The Johns Hopkins Unversity

EQUALITY AND THE RIGHTS OF WOMEN. By Elizabeth H. Wolgast. *Ithaca, N.Y. Cornell University Press, 1980. Pp. 176. Index. Bibliography. $12.50.*

A mistake commonly made in arguments about sex roles and the rights of women is the conflation of child rearing with child bearing. Woman's greater part in physical reproduction is held to imply her greater responsibility, or suitability, for all that goes into raising children to adulthood. The argument of Elizabeth Wolgast's new book, *Equality and Women's Rights,* is based upon an unusual variant of this fallacy. Picking up on the "uncertainty of paternity" factor—which Hume regarded as justification for the double sexual standard and Rousseau used to legitimize the total subordination of women—Wolgast uses it to argue against an egalitarian or androgynous position on women's rights.

The result is a curious and disappointing book on a subject that deserves better treatment. The arguments are frequently loose, the representation of the views of others is often inadequate or oversimplified, and the usage of generally understood terms is on several occasions so odd that the reader has difficulty following the discussion. It is extraordinary, too, to find a philosopher who advocates the greater representation of the views of women as well as men "in [our] very conception of what society is" (p. 158), persisiting in the traditional usage of words like "he" and "men" when she is clearly referring to persons of both sexes. Quite apart from the fact that in a book about the equality or lack of it between the sexes such linguistic sexism causes ambiguity, its rejection must surely be one of the very first steps away from a male dominated view of human society.

The book's main defect, however, is that the foundation for its argument that women should have certain special rights (as well as many rights shared equally with men) is a claim neither convincing nor consistent with the author's own political world view. Wolgast's argument is based on the claim that mothers are necessarily the "primary parents" of their children. This is due, she asserts, to the fact that: "a woman does not normally have occasion to wonder whether the baby she bears is hers. She does not wonder if she or someone else is the mother. The father stands in a different relation to his child at the outset. . . "(p. 25). This inherent asymmetry of parenthood means that mothers have a place as parents "that cannot be occupied by a father," and that the potential of pregnancy and motherhood is "part of a young female's life and thought in a way they [sic] cannot be for a male" (p. 26-27). The significant asymmetries of parenthood, moreover, will affect other aspects of men's and women's lives, "some only indirectly related to parenthood" (p. 28). Among other things, these asymmetrics mean that the mother and the father of a child cannot relate to each other as peers, and that women must have special rights not shared by men.

We must seriously question the premise that leads to all these conclusions. First, granted that the possibility of mistaken biological paternity exists, do fathers *normally* wonder any more than mothers whether their children are their own? For the critical issue, surely, is not that of mere possibility, but rather of whether men's real doubts about their children's paternity are prevalent enough to affect father/child relations throughout society. Wolgast gives no evidence at all on the latter and I strongly suspect that men's doubts are not so prevalent.

Second, the argument depends upon the assumption that not only biological parenthood, but the absolute certainty of it, are the crucial factors in making people into parents. If this were the case, one must be most pessimistic about the quality of care that adopted children could ever receive, since it is certain in their case that they are *not* the biological children of their parents. Yet in most cases this seems to have little effect on their adoptive parents' attachment to them, or on the quality of care these children receive.

The strangest aspect of Wolgast's use of the argument from the uncertainty of paternity as a basis for social distinction between the sexes is that it is so much at odds with her own stated views of human relations, especially relations within families. The notion that doubt about paternity is a significant factor in parent/child relations, and therefore in the assignment of sex roles, implies a generally high level of distrust and hostility between men and women, even in their most intimate and committed relations with each other. It also suggests that narcissistic identification or biological possession is the most important factor determining parents' attachment to their children. But such a Hobbesian view of human relations is poles apart from the view that Wolgast herself adopts. For she characterizes both parent/child and husband/wife relations as essentially founded on *trust*, to the extent that abuses of this trust "vitiate the very roles" (p. 73). Surely, though a fairly basic degree of trust between a husband and a wife suffices to save the former from doubting his children's paternity? In the final chapter, which is by far the most worthwhile section of the book, Wolgast attacks atomistic conceptions which view society as a simple collection of self-interested and autonomous individuals. She argues for a model of political life that allows for connections and interdependencies amongst persons other than the self-interested ones of the atomistic liberal model. Within the family specifically, she asserts, people often act in non-self-interested ways, responding to the needs of others even when to do so interferes with satisfaction of their own wants. Her argument that the possessive individualism of most liberal thought cannot satisfactorily account for family relations is a good one. Yet Wolgast seems completely unaware of the tension that so clearly exists between the model she suggests as an alternative and her previous argument. If the extent of distrust that leads to real doubt about paternity is a permanent and general aspect of the human condition, how can one reasonably expect that family members will relate to each other in any but a self-interested manner?

If Wolgast's argument about the necessary asymmetry of parenthood fails, the special rights she claims for women have no basis, and she is left without a case against feminists who argue for equal rights for women. Indeed, the special rights that she mentions specifically are either harmful to women's long term interests, because of their tendency to preserve stereotypes, or else they can be subsumed under general rights, held by all. Pregnancy and childbirth can and should be treated by law and public policy in the same way as any other physical condition requiring health care and time for recuperation. Their exclusion or differential treatment clearly constitute sex discrimination, however the Supreme Court may contort itself in order to conclude otherwise. As for child care, if we are to achieve a non-sexist society both parents must have the opportunity to share equally in it, and the relevant rights (for example the right to parenthood leave during early infancy, or the right for a parent of a young child to work less than full-time) must belong to parents regardless of sex. As for the type of special rights that have been granted women in order to compensate for their years out of the paid labor force, even now, these rights would be far more equitably assigned in accordance with need than on the basis of sex. Moreover, the sooner parenthood is truly shared, the sooner this particular aspect of women's vulnerability will become obsolete. Finally, is there any reason at all why society should provide less support for motherless children than fatherless ones?—again, provided that economic need is taken into account.

Wolgast asks why women are so under-represented in many professions and important positions but, significantly, she omits one of the most obvious reasons of all—that they, and not men, have carried the full responsibility (as well as enjoying more of the pleasures) of parenthood. Only the abandonment of the unfounded notion that women must be their children's primary parents, together with the introduction of considerable flexibility into the world of work, will enable women to share equally with men in influencing the world from both inside and outside the home.

Susan Moller Okin
Brandeis University

BOOKS COMMISSIONED FOR REVIEW

Brownlee, W. and M. *Women in the American Economy, A Documentary History, 1675 to 1929*
Cantarow, E. *Moving the Mountain*
Chambers, D. *Making Fathers Pay: the Enforcement of Child Support*
Chaney, E. *Supermadre*
Cummings, B., V. Schuck. *Women Organizing: An Anthology*
Evans, S. *Personal Politics*
Feinstein, K. ed. *Working Women and Families*
Gelles, R. *Family Violence*
Howard, S. *But We Will Persist*
Kohn, W. *Women in National Legislatures*
Kurian, George, ed. *Cross-Cultural Perspectives on Mate-Selection and Marriage*
La Frances Rodgers, R., ed. *The Black Woman*
Lagemann, E. *A Generation of Women: Education in the Lives of Progressive Reformers*
Lavrin, A., ed. *Latin American Women: Historical Perspectives*
Mandle, J. *Women and Social Change in America*
Mirand, A., and E. Enriquez. *La Chicana: the Mexican-American Woman*
Nash, J., and H. Safa, eds. *Sex and Class in Latin America*
Ratner, R., ed. *Equal Employment for Women*
Robinson, L. *Sex, Class, and Culture*
Sabrovsky, J. *From Rationality to Liberation, The Evolution of Feminist Ideology*
Scharf, L. *To Work and To Wed*
Sherman, J., and E. Beck. *The Prism of Sex*
Smith, R., ed. *The Subtle Revolution, Women at Work*
Spiro, M.E. *Gender and Culture: Kibbutz Women Revisited*
Stencel, S. *The Changing American Family*
Trescott, M., ed. *Dynamos and Virgins Revisited: Women and Technological Change in History*
Tufte, V., and B. Myerhoff. eds. *Changing Images of the Family*
Unger, R. *Female and Male*
Warren, M. A. *The Nature of Woman, An Encyclopedia and Guide to the Literature*
Weitzman, L. *Sex Role Socialization*
Williamson, J. *New Feminist Scholarship, A Guide to Bibliographies*
Yohalem, A. *The Careers of Professional Women, Commitment and Conflict*

BOOKS RECEIVED

Adams, C., and K. Winston. *Mothers at Work: Public Policies in the United States, Sweden and China*

Berk, S., ed. *Women and Household Labor*

Berkin, C. and C. Lovett, eds. *Women, War and Revolution*

Center for Educational Research and Innovation, *Child and Family, Demographic Developments in the OECD Countries*

Clements, B. *Bolshevik Feminist: The Life of Aleksandra Kollontai*

Gage, M. *Woman, Church and State: The Original Expose of Male Collaboration Against the Female Sex*

Hill, M. *Charlotte Perkins Gilman: The Making of a Radical Feminist, 1860-1896*

Kamerman, S. and A. Kahn, eds. *Family Policy: Government and Families in Fourteen Countries*

Lamson, P. *In the Vanguard: Six American Women in Public Life*

Lapidus, G. *Women in Soviet Society: Equality, Development, and Social Change*

Sacks, K. *Sisters and Wives: The Past and Future of Sexual Equality*

Weekes-Vagliani, W. *Women in Development*

instructions for authors

SUBMISSION OF MANUSCRIPTS. Manuscripts, together with an abstract of about 100 words, should be submitted to the Editor (see second page of issue for address) in triplicate, and must include a stamped, self-addressed postcard containing the manuscript title for acknowledgment of receipt. In addition, authors should include a self-addressed 9 × 12'' envelope with sufficient postage to insure return of the manuscript.

PREPARATION. Articles must be typed on one side of clean, 8½ × 11'' white bond paper with a one-inch margin on all four sides. Except under unusual circumstances, manuscript length should be approximately 20 double-spaced pages. The abstract should precede the text on a separate piece of paper. The entire manuscript, including abstract, quotations, tables, and references, must be double-spaced. Authors are advised that *no revisions* of the manuscript can be made after acceptance by the Editor for publication.

ANONYMOUS REVIEW. To facilitate anonymous review by one or more readers, *only the title of the article* should appear on the first page of the manuscript. An attached cover page must contain the title, authorship, and an introductory footnote with the authors' professional titles, academic degrees, mailing addresses, and any statements of credit or research support. Any reference to authors in the text or footnotes should be placed on a separate sheet of paper and not in the text.

TABLES AND FIGURES. All tables and figures must be submitted in camera-ready form. That is, only original typescript, drawings, or glossy prints suitable for reproduction, may be submitted. Photocopied material, blue ink, pencil, or hand-drawn lettering are not acceptable. Figures must be prepared using black India ink and professional drawing instruments. Type all figure legends double-spaced on a separate sheet of paper and place at the end of the manuscript. Tables and figures should be numbered separately using Arabic numerals, and placed together at the end of the manuscript. Provide brief notes within the text to indicate where each table and figure is to appear. Write the article title and table or figure number lightly in pencil on the back of each item.

STYLE. Over all style should conform to that found within these pages and outlined in the latest edition of the University of Chicago Manual of Style. The use of overly long or numerous insets is discouraged. Words should be underlined only when it is intended that they be typeset in *italics.* Long articles, or articles containing complex material should be broken up by short, meaningful subheadings.

REFERENCES. Footnotes must be organized in the order presented and appended to the conclusion of the text. The reference section must be double-spaced. All works referred to in the text must be included in the reference section; all references must have in-text citations. Do not use abbreviations for journal titles. For further information concerning the preparation of references, consult the brochure, "Information for Authors," available from the Editor or the latest edition of the University of Chicago Manual of Style.

ORIGINALITY. Authors should note that only original articles are accepted for publication. Submission of a manuscript represents certification on the part of the author(s) that neither the article submitted nor a version of it has been published, nor is being considered for publication elsewhere. Such articles may be published only by permission of the Editor.

REPRINTS. About three weeks after publication, 10 free reprints will be mailed to senior authors. All authors will receive information for ordering additional reprints.